Hypocrisy
and Self-Deception
in Hawthorne's Fiction

Hypocrisy
and Self-Deception
in Hawthorne's Fiction

KENNETH MARC HARRIS

University Press of Virginia
Charlottesville

To my parents,
Jess and Freda Harris

THE UNIVERSITY PRESS OF VIRGINIA
Copyright © 1988 by the Rector and Visitors
of the University of Virginia

First published 1988

Library of Congress Cataloging-in-Publication Data

Harris, Kenneth Marc, 1948–
    Hypocrisy and self-deception in Hawthorne's fiction.

    Includes index.
    1. Hawthorne, Nathaniel, 1804–1864—Criticism and
interpretation. 2. Hypocrisy in literature.
3. Self-deception in literature. I. Title.
PS1892.H94H37   1988   813'.3   87-25403
ISBN   0-8139-1172-9

Design by Diane Nelson
Composition by Keystone Typesetting
Printed by Thomson-Shore, Inc.
Bound by John H. Dekker & Sons, Inc.

Printed in the United States of America

Contents

"The Age of Hypocrisy"

In a brilliant essay, "Let Us Not Be Hypocritical," Judith Shklar characterizes the modern (that is, the post–French Revolution) era as the "age of hypocrisy." By this she does not really mean that we are collectively less honest or more calculating than were our premodern ancestors. Rather, she claims we live in a "culture of hypocrisy" such that only two possibilities are open to us and both necessarily entail bad faith. Her models, or archetypes, for the two possibilities are derived from Molière, the preeminent artist of hypocrisy. On the one hand there is conscious hypocrisy as embodied in Tartuffe, the knowing dissembler. But there is also what Shklar calls the "antihypocrisy" of Alceste, which is no less reprehensible because it leads inevitably to misanthropy. Indeed, the two qualities are not at all the polar opposites the terms imply, inasmuch as when the hypocrite and the antihypocrite are brought together (as they increasingly are in contemporary life, according to Shklar), it becomes evident that "each one, to some extent, shares as much as detests the inclinations of the other." That is because the "new hypocrisy makes sincerity its central virtue," so that both hypocrites and antihypocrites "measure the distance between assertion and performance [in each other's behavior] and both say, 'Hypocrisy.'"[1]

Shklar proceeds with her social criticism on the basis of a wide range of observations of modern life and culture; however, the impressive philosophical scaffolding for her analysis is erected largely on the ground laid out in the account of hypocrisy given in part C of chapter 6 of Hegel's *Phenomenology*. Even for a German philosopher Hegel is notoriously murky in his style of writing (at least), and so it is probably significant in itself that nothing in all his works is communicated with greater clarity than his abhorrence of hypocrisy in that section. "It has to be made manifest that it *is* evil," reads a particularly virulent and uncharacteristically pithy sentence, "and its objective existence thus made congruent with its real nature; the hypocrisy must be unmasked." He goes so far as to revise La Rochefoucauld's familiar maxim that hypocrisy is the compliment vice pays to virtue by suggesting that the purported compliment is actually an insult, because "there is really implied its own contempt for that inherent principle [of virtue]." Hypocrisy is utterly evil because, in adopting the semblance of virtue, it robs virtue of all vitality, substance, and value: "For what lets itself be used as an external instrument shows itself to be a thing, which has within it no proper weight of its own."[2]

Unfortunately, his explanation of hypocrisy is not so readily comprehensible as his detestation of its supposed ubiquity. For my purpose it should suffice to say that Hegel's theory of hypocrisy cannot be separated from his overall philosophical system, according to which the conditions now favorable to epidemic hypocrisy will be superseded as Spirit advances through history. Judith Shklar similarly, though less metaphysically, holds out hope for our eventually recovering the possibility of genuine candor. However, according to another Hegelian scholar's interpretation of part C of chapter 6 of the *Phenomenology,* it would be difficult to see how anyone could ever escape the contagion. As Jonathan Robinson reads Hegel and applies his thinking to contemporary life, such are the moral and psychological complexities of modern social organization that it is not the man or woman of weak or evil character who would be most suspect, but, on the contrary, it is "a person trying to live a life based on the idea of duty [who] will end up a hypocrite."[3] Robinson's understanding of Hegel's position is not fundamentally different from Shklar's, merely darker. He might have mentioned (although he doesn't) Alceste as an example of a "dutiful" hypocrite. (Instead he discusses Robert McNamara's conduct during the Vietnam War!)

In his fiction Nathaniel Hawthorne depicts both quasi-angelic though shallow individuals whose sincerity is beyond question, and psychologically richer though in some way defective characters who fall victims to bad faith yet ultimately reclaim their integrity.

Nevertheless, despite these significant exceptions, I find his work, taken as a whole, a rendering of the human condition much closer to Robinson's gloomier Hegelian assessment than to Shklar's more hopeful prognosis. A census of all the inhabitants of Hawthorne's imagined world would certainly result in the finding that the overwhelming majority are hypocrites, self-deceivers, or both. Moreover, only a handful from this great populace of the insincere are designing frauds like Westervelt, and these are not especially important characters. By and large, most fit the more problematic pattern of Hollingsworth, living what they see as lives of duty, or at least of rectitude, yet ending up as hypocrites. Furthermore, this group includes many of his major figures. While it is also true that almost all these major figures come to recognize, however belatedly, their bad faith and to leave us with some hope, however faint, that they may reform, nonetheless their redemption could more convincingly be ascribed to the conventions of moralistic romance than to the author's seriously holding out the prospect of society in general having a rebirth into sincerity and truthfulness. There is no suggestion, for example, that the pious Christian matrons who call for Hester's execution or the Pyncheon neighbors who fulfill their civic obligations by spying for the Judge will ever become aware, much less admit, that their behavior is based on a double standard. If Dimmesdale, on the other hand, really does escape the maze of self-delusion, it may simply be because he is the hero of a romance and not because human beings actually can learn to be honest with themselves. The mass of people in Hawthorne's stories, who are not romance heroes, lead lives of hypocrisy and self-deception. Presumably, most of the rest of us, who are not heroes of romance either, would in Hawthorne's view be condemned to languish in the same Hegelian predicament.

Be that as it may, my concern is not with Hawthorne's opinions per se on hypocrisy and self-deception but with the meaning of hypocrisy and self-deception in his fictions and with the manner of their functioning in his artistry. Among major literary artists for whom hypocrisy is a significant theme, Shklar ranks Hawthorne behind Molière only (and ahead of Ibsen and Dickens). Yet while virtually every critic of Hawthorne has commented to some extent on the prominence of hypocrisy in much of his work, there has been no in-depth study of this theme taken in isolation, and one of my goals is to remedy that deficiency. Accordingly, my book has a bulge in its center, with the two central chapters devoted to *The Scarlet Letter.* I hope to demonstrate that, if hypocrisy and self-deception are not the very essence of Hawthorne's masterpiece, at least they are *at* the very essence and could not be easily separated from any reasonable account of the essence. The preceding chapter, on the short fiction, and the following chapter, on *The House of the Seven Gables*, are intended to show, among other things, the gradual building up of Hawthorne's interest in hypocrisy and self-deception in the period before *The Scarlet Letter* and the slow winding down or at least leveling off of it afterwards as he begins to turn in new directions.

Another of my goals is to suggest where the preoccupation with hypocrisy and self-deception in Hawthorne's fiction may have come from. No one has addressed that question to my knowledge, perhaps on the assumption that it was simply a peculiarity of Hawthorne's mind, and no doubt to some degree it was. Certainly it did not come from Hegel. Yet just as Molière's obsession with hypocrisy can be related to the frequent recurrence of the theme in earlier French thought and culture,[4] so Hawthorne's comparable preoccupations might reasonably be supposed to have antecedents in earlier American life and letters, especially in view of his well-known fascination with local history. I strongly believe, though I cannot claim to have absolutely proved, that Hawthorne's hypocrites and self-deceivers ultimately tract their thematic ancestry from the remarkable efforts of Puritan clergymen in colonial New England to establish criteria for detecting impostor saints (both conscious and unconscious) in their congregations and even among themselves. To that end, I begin with a chapter that, after briefly placing the general Puritan attitude toward the problem in historical perspective, goes on to examine some of the more interesting theological approaches that were devised by various Puritan thinkers to solve it. It should subsequently become apparent how far the psychological circumstances and moral dilemmas of many of Hawthorne's characters might be regarded as secular equivalents, within the conventions of romance, to the predicament of an old Puritan bête noire, what I like to call the self-deceiving hypocrite. Thus in *The House of the Seven Gables* the almost literal reincarnation of one such bête noire becomes the butt of a comic melodrama.

Elsewhere the fictional situation is more ambiguous, in keeping with the complexity of the original Puritan conception of the problem.

In addition to explaining what it is and speculating on where it came from, I also hope to indicate where Hawthorne's interest in hypocrisy and self-deception leads in terms of his artistic development. A current trend in Hawthorne criticism emphasizes the growing self-consciousness of his artistry as his career progresses. Using Kierkegaard's distinction between hypocrisy and irony, I try to show how a key turning point in this process occurs in *The Blithedale Romance.* In that book the moral and psychological dilemmas of the major characters, which are consistent with the themes of hypocrisy and self-deception as carried over from the earlier work, are subsumed by an ironic and self-consciously artful narrator into the conventions of romantic fiction. At this point the issue of hypocrisy and self-deception, in and of itself, has effectively been resolved for Hawthorne, but in a postscript I briefly examine an interesting related issue pertaining to his last completed novel. Ultimately, my aim is to persuade students of Hawthorne that hypocrisy and self-deception should be added to the list of recognized Hawthornian themes such as illusion and reality or art and life because it amplifies the central Hawthornian position. We are unable to transcend our human limitations, perhaps not even through art, but at least in art we can sometimes deceive ourselves with the saving illusion that we might.

Hypocrisy
and Self-Deception
in Hawthorne's Fiction

ONE

Hypocrisy and the New England Way

T HE HISTORY of the word *hypocrisy* goes back to classic theater, perhaps to the very beginning of Greek drama, when an individual speaker (*hypokritēs*) was first separated from the previously un-differentiated chorus and made to "speak under" (*hypokrinesthai*) their ritualistic chant. We still tend to adopt the language of the theater when describing the behavior of a hypocrite, who we say is "playing a role" or, like an ancient actor, "wearing a mask" or even being "two-faced." At its very origin, then, the concept of hypoc-risy involves a fundamental confusion or ambiguity between reality and illusion and between life and art. Another important attribute of hypocrisy has Judaic rather than classic sources, and that is the taint of wickedness associated with hypocrisy but not with other forms of "playacting." The Greek word *hypokritēs* appeared fre-quently in literature of the Jewish dispersion with reference to evil, and in the Septuagint it was used to translate the Hebrew *hōnep* or *hānep*, meaning "be polluted, profane, godless," which is found in several books of the Old Testament, particularly in Job.[1] In this form the word passed into the New Testament, where, as a biblical scholar explains, "the terms [*hypokrisis* and *hypokritēs*] are invariably evil in sense," thus providing "our English transliterations of the terms ('hypocrisy,' 'hypocrite') the persistent meaning of 'pretend-ing to be what one is not,' especially in the areas of religion and morality."[2] The word, then, comes down to us with two quite distinct yet inseparable connotations. The first connotation is on-tological and raises the question of what constitutes a person's real self. The second connotation is moral: we distinguish hypocrisy

1

from other occasions when a person might project an appearance at variance from his true nature—as on the legitimate stage, for instance, or in the case of a pathological delusion—by directly ascribing evil to the hypocrite, but not to the stage actor or to the madman, for practicing his deception.

This dual connotation may be illustrated by the hypocrites Dante describes in canto 23 of the *Inferno*. They bear the heavy weight of moral odium carried by hypocrites in the medieval period literally in the form of gilded monkish cloaks lined with lead. It is a kind of theatrical costume that disguises the true nature of the wearers, but at the same time it punishes and mocks them. Similarly, they are said to be a "painted people," which echoes both Christ's condemnation of hypocrites as "whited sepulchres" (Matthew 23:27) and Isidore of Seville's derivation of the word *hypocrite* from actors in stage makeup, a faulty etymology that Thomas Aquinas draws on. They speak of themselves to Dante and Vergil as "sad hypocrites," again in illusion to Matthew (6:16), where Christ accuses the hypocrites of disfiguring their faces so "that they may appear unto men to fast"—which raises the ontological question because now, in hell, the sadness of their faces is no longer a hypocritical mask but rather a truthful expression of their utter despair.[3] At the same time the moral connotation is further emphasized by Dante's placing among the hypocrites Caiaphas, the Jewish high priest who approved of Christ's execution (John 11:49–52), and giving him one of the most extreme punishments in the entire poem, an eternal crucifixion.

My account of hypocrisy thus far as an amalgam of illusion and deceit would be roughly serviceable for most hypocrites encountered in Western literature down to the time of Shakespeare and even Molière, but if we were to take it much beyond that a third element would have to be added. "The hypocrite-villain, the conscious dissembler," as Lionel Trilling writes in *Sincerity and Authenticity*, "has become marginal, even alien, to the modern imagination." Unless we are contemplating a transcendent literary text, such as *Othello* or *The Misanthrope* (and to some degree even then), the machinations of a calculating hypocrite fail to "readily command our interest, scarcely our credence." Yet in a modified form hypocrisy, or perhaps we might say some other quality that has evolved from hypocrisy, continues to exert a power to fascinate us.

2   "The deception we best understand," as Trilling puts it, "and most

willingly give our attention to is that which a person works upon himself."[4] In addition to theatrical illusiveness and unmitigated evil, the third element in the modern conception of hypocrisy is self-deception, and in this form it can be seen as even more pervasive in society and in culture than was the simpler hypocrisy that preceded it and is now all but obsolete. Thus understood as bad faith or self-decption, it "might almost be considered the preoccupation of modern literature," as a recent commentator suggests.[5]

In the past twenty-five years there has been a steady surge of interest in self-deception, not so much among literary critics as from philosophers and psychologists, mainly American and British. For the most part I will ignore their investigations as irrelevant to my present concerns, although, as will be seen, I find the account of the mechanism of self-deception offered by Herbert Fingarette illuminating with regard to the behavior of certain Hawthornian self-deceivers. Most of the remainder of these recent studies, however, are too theoretical and abstract to be of use. Two points concerning them, though, deserve to be mentioned briefly if only to set out the distance between self-deception as it was viewed in Hawthorne's time and the ways in which it is being revaluated now. First, it is now very much an open question whether such a thing as self-deception exists. The 1960 essay by Raphael Demos that apparently initiated the current vogue presented self-deception as an irreducible paradox: "that B believes both p and not -p at the same time." Accordingly, most studies have sought to circumvent the paradox either by modifying the formula or by flatly denying its application to anything conceivable.[6] Formerly, though, it was accepted uncritically that anyone could in fact deceive himself and that indeed we often do. Second, in the current debate it is unsettled whether self-deception should be approached as a moral issue rather than as a morally neutral matter of phenomenological concern to psychologists or logicians or linguists. A related issue is whether self-deception is necessarily evil, and some writers have gone so far as to propose a morally positive, or at least an "innocent" self-deception or even a "self-deceptive faith."[7] Until this century not only was the evil of self-deception taken for granted, but it was also widely viewed as terribly evil, or even as supremely evil, as when Matthew Arnold grandiloquently proclaimed in 1870 that "than self-deceit there is nothing by nature more baneful," or when a decade later Father Zossima advised Fyodor Pavlovitch in *The Brothers Karamazov*, "Above all, don't lie to yourself."[8] Of the two major figures from the earlier twentieth century most frequently cited in contemporary studies of self-deception, Freud, in the moral dimension of his thought, is problematic, but Sartre, in his theory of bad faith, is notoriously moralistic.[9]

Admittedly, it would be difficult to prove, and yet it seems quite possible that the moral obloquy traditionally attached to self-deception results from its long and intimate association with hypocrisy. Francis Bacon wrote of hypocrites in his *Meditationes Sacrae* (1597), "There are some however of a deeper and more inflated hypocrisy, who deceiving themselves, and fancying themselves worthy of a closer conversation with God, neglect the duties of charity towards their neighbour, as inferior matters."[10] In view of Bacon's personal history, his greater contempt for hypocrites who are also self-deceivers is perhaps best understood in the context of Renaissance standards of conduct regarding the life of the courtier, in whom an ability to dissemble skillfully was considered a political asset.[11] Nonetheless, Bacon's sentence also pithily captures the moral oddity of self-deceiving hypocrisy as the idea is developed later, first by English and then more elaborately by American Puritans, for it is preciesely in the objective sinner's subjective assurance of his sanctity that the essence of the evil resides, rather than in his immoral deeds or even in his more patently hypocritical behavior. The unregenerate sinner's presumption that he is "worthy of a closer conversation with God" is his foulest abomination against God.

There used to be a tendency among modern students of Puritanism to assume that Puritan congregations considered themselves in theory to be comprised of the elect, although in practice acknowledging that some reprobates would inevitably slip in. A revised view more recently offered by John S. Coolidge in *The Pauline Renaissance in England* is that the Puritans accepted the unregenerate into Church membership, not as "a regrettable compromise with the conditions of life in this world," but rather as "essential" to the composition of the church according to the divine plan. "To attempt to exclude them [the unregenerate] would not be merely impractical," Coolidge continues, "it would be a denial of the identity of the Church with the chosen people of the Old Testament," which similarly included several less than perfectly upright figures, like Saul.[12] Moreover, just as someone like Saul occasionally would have felt himself to be in God's favor, so an unregenerate church member might also believe himself sanctified. This is a matter of vital importance to us, because it explains the Puritan's preoccupation with what I call self-deceiving hypocrisy; furthermore, it goes to the core of Puritan doctrine. As Calvin puts it in a passage from the *Institutes* excerpted by Coolidge, "The reprobate are sometimes affected by almost the same feeling as the elect, so that *even in their own judgment* they do not in any way differ from the elect" (emphasis added).[13] As a result of their self-deception they may perform some good in the world, or at least think they do, but they remain unregenerate simply because, regardless of their impressions, in fact they are not in a state of grace. Indeed, Calvin quickly goes on to suggest that God's actual purpose in giving them "a taste of the heavenly gifts" is "to render them more convicted and inexcusable." But that does not mean that the heavenly taste in the mouths of these particular reprobates is in some way delusive. The Lord never deals in bogus merchandise, nor is he an Indian giver. What it actually is the reprobates get a taste of, a taste sweet enough to make them confident of their election, constitutes a problem. Calvin's conception of "common" graces provides part of an answer, but these qualities, as the term implies, are little more than ordinary accomplishments (a knack for preaching, clean living, temperance, etc.), with little of the supernatural about them. Hardly enough to account for the reprobates' fatal self-deception.

According to Coolidge, it was John Cotton who came closest to solving the problem by extending Calvin's "common" graces to what Cotton called "federal" grace, which, explains Coolidge, "is evidently intended to clarify a question which Calvin never clearly addresses himself to: what, precisely, is holy about those persons who are 'accounted an holy seed' [that is, are admitted to communion] although predestined to reprobation?" In essence, Cotton's solution distinguishes the grace granted an individual for his personal salvation from the grace dispensed by God to his church collectively. Cotton agrees with Calvin that the holiness accrued by the (unaware) reprobate is of no benefit to him whatever; on the contrary, it may even add to his guilt, because, Calvin admonishes, "by handling something sacred, the unclean hand profanes it." Nonetheless, good may be produced through the reprobate as a medium, so to speak, accruing holiness for the faithful corporately. 5

That the reprobate deceives himself into regarding this "federal" grace as saving grace for him personally is attributable, presumably, to the treachery of his heart. In any case, it must be part of God's plan for such people to exist: "Cotton does not hesitate to conclude from the Covenant with Abraham," Coolidge bluntly sums up, "that God sanctifies hypocrisy in the seed of Abraham."[14]

In order to demonstrate how Cotton's reinterpretation of Covenant theology through the idea of "federal" grace enabled him to tolerate all sorts of reprobates in the visible church, Coolidge goes on to discuss Cotton's well-known quasi parable about swine and goats. The witty little sketch can also serve as a preliminary illustration of the complexity and profundity of Puritan thinking on hypocrisy.

Cotton divides hypocrites into two categories (both of which, he adds parenthetically, "you shall find . . . in the Church of God"): "washed Swine" and "Goats."[15] The swine are "the grosser kind of Hypocrites" who from time to time renounce their porcine ways but without really meaning it and inevitably return to their former habits, "as a Swine when he cometh where the puddle is, will readily lye down in it." The goats, on the other hand, "goe far beyond these" and present a much knottier problem for the zoologists of hypocrisy: "these are clean Beasts such as chew the cudd, meditate upon Ordinances, and they divide the hoofe, they live both in a generall and particular calling, and will not be idle; they are also fit for sacrifice; what then is wanting?" In other words, how can you tell them apart from the sheep?

Cotton's answer to this question never drops the farm animal analogy, but despite its Aesopian charm it touches upon some disturbing issues regarding the Puritan hypocrite. "The Goat is of a Capricious nature," he punningly begins, "and affecteth Eminency, his gate also is stately." Eschewing the swine's transparently hypocritical pretense at compunction and self-reformation, the goats exhibit a genuine zeal for purity: paradoxically, it is through their very overzealousness that their hypocrisy betrays them. While the sheep sheepishly submit to Christ's shepherding with self-effacing humility, the goats "are full of Ambition, they cannot abide swamps and holes, but will be climbing upon the tops of mountains," as if they could find the way to heaven on their own. Yet for all their care not to dirty themselves, they are "rankish" creatures, particularly the "old Goats" with "their unsavory relish."

6

Translating this into human terms, we get something like the following. Tartuffe-like hyprocrites, who consciously play the role of pious church members as the means of accomplishing various evil strategems, should not be tolerated once they have been exposed. But, there are others whose presence is not only acceptable but even beneficial to the church as a whole. One such class of hypocrites is comprised of the perpetual backsliders, who always resolve never to slip again but do so at the earliest opportunity. Eventually, one might suppose, their hypocrisy would become apparent to everyone else, if not to themselves. But there are others who strive with their entire being for salvation. They yearn for God's love, and their every effort is keyed to winning God's favor. Yet they will never be saved, because their very nature makes them hateful to God regardless of what they do, what they say, what they think, or what they feel. In fact, the closer they seek to approach to God, the more repulsive he finds them. And even if it were possible to know this about themselves, they would be helpless to alter their predicament. Goats can't be changed into sheep.

Exploring the nature of hypocrisy was an important theoretical task in early New England because detecting hypocrites was an urgent practical matter. The peculiar colonial program of "testing prospective members of the church for signs of saving grace, and thus attempting to make the visible church a spiritual approximation of the invisible church,"[16] while it may not have been quite so prevalent or rigorous as Edmund S. Morgan contends,[17] would of necessity have involved exposing hypocrisy, especially the more subtle forms arising from self-deception. In addition, just as the formal trying of candidates for a reasonable presumption of sainthood was, according to Morgan, a homegrown practice, so it would seem from the sheer volume of writing on the subject that hypocrite-hunting also became a New England specialty.

It might not be too great an overstatement to say it became a New England obsession. As is well known, one of the main points of contention in the famous controversy between Cotton and Roger Williams was the excommunication of hypocrites.[18] As we have seen, Cotton didn't believe it was practicable to try to exclude hypocrites from the saints' congregations or even necessarily desirable. As he put it in his livestock parable, "You may receive a Goat into Church-fellowship for all his capricious nature, and he will be a clean creature, and of much good use."[19] Williams's insistence that exclusion was indispensable regardless of the difficulty (a position that eventually helped drive him to radical toleration) can be seen as occupying the other end of a continuum from Cotton's acceptance of the hypocrites for their usefulness. Because they are at the extremes, neither Cotton nor Williams developed the elaborate theories and intricate schemes of classification we encounter among New England theologians who took a middle position— that it was both worthwhile and realistic to detect at least some hypocrites, including self-deceiving hypocrites. I touch on just the more interesting schemes and theories to provide some idea of the extent to which hypocrisy was a matter of concern in early colonial New England. As we shall see, it is all closely tied in with what Coolidge aptly calls "the whole casuistry of religious affections which characterizes the last phase of Puritanism."[20]

So aware of the great complexity of the problem was the systematic and compendious Samuel Willard that his ecclesiastical strictures entail a caution to beware of self-deception not only for the hypocrites but also for those who would expose the hypocrisy of others. In withdrawing communion from purported sinners, we should make certain we have not been so misled by "jealousy" as "to put a sinister interpretation upon their best and most laudable actions as if they proceeded from a false heart." This amounts to warning us not to become hypocrites ourselves by falsely attributing hypocrisy elsewhere, although Willard concedes that in the final analysis one never really knows beyond all doubt who is and who is not a hypocrite. "The differencing notes by which sincerity and hypocrisy are to be distinguished are latent," Willard admonishes. "God only knows them certainly."[21]

Thomas Hooker was more optimistic about the feasibility of identifying and uprooting the seeds of hypocrisy and of thereby assisting those who may unknowingly fall into self-deception. Thus in order to help believers "ascertain the validity of their vocation," as Phyllis and Nicholas Jones explain, Hooker sketches in *The Soul's Vocation* (1637–38) an extensive rogues' gallery of hypocrites: "the lazy hypocrite, the stage hypocrite, the terrified hypocrite, the whining hypocrite, the sturdy hypocrite, the glorious hypocrite, the presumptuous hypocrite, the shifting hypocrite, and the stately hypocrite." But though the number of categories is impressive, it is apparent from the superficiality of the treatments that Hooker is merely compiling caricatures, not attempting a serious classification. His cartoon hypocrites seem much less human than Cotton's menagerie of sheep, swine, and goats. Hooker seizes upon love as a criterion for verifying one's sanctity; he recognizes, however, the need to "discover the difference" between divinely inspired love and "all the feigned and false love and joy, which hypocrites pretend to have, and seem to express to the Lord Jesus Christ."[22] Significantly, he offers Judas as an example of the latter variety, indicating, if nothing else, the high degree of wickedness the Puritans, like all Christians, attach to hypocrisy.

Indeed, in describing what he calls "gospel" or "evangelical" hypocrites, Thomas Shepard tentatively identifies what we have been referring to as self-deceiving hypocrisy with "the unpardonable sin." "Many a man laies claim to Christ and his Blood, that never knew the worth of it," he explains, "and this is Christs complaint methinks in Heaven, (and of Saints on earth) He comes unto his own, and his own esteem him not, his own love him not, his own receive him not."[23] Shepard's *Parable of the Ten Virgins* (1660) deserves some extra attention from us because it is the most profound statement of the Puritan conception of self-deceiving hypocrisy and also because it is noteworthy among all treatments of hypocrisy for its depth of psychological insight.

In his clerical career Shepard seems gradually to have shifted from being an uncompromising ferret of hypocrites and self-deceivers—he once refused to authorize a new church because the founders had misjudged their own conversion—to an acceptance of hypocrites under a conception of "federal" holiness like Cotton's.[24] In his private life, however, his pursuit of hypocrisy was unremitting, and the hypocrite he was chasing was himself. "On Sabbath when I came home," reads a representative passage from his Journal for 1641, "I saw the hypocrisy of my heart that in my ministry I sought to comfort others and quicken others that the glory might reflect on me as well as on God." This lifelong conviction of his hypocritical inner nature can be traced back at least to his first brush with Puritanism, at age eighteen, when he heard (in England) a sermon by John Preston that, as he recalled in his *Autobiography*, laid open "the hypocrisy of all my good things I thought I had in me . . . all the turnings and deceits of my heart . . . my hypocrisy and self and secret sins."[25]

Naturally, the accomplishment of his conversion only served in

9

the long run to increase his suspicions about its validity. Like Hooker and others, Shepard had his methods for distinguishing "the difference between affections of Saints and Hypocrites of Christ," but his main criterion, though logically coherent, would be more likely to heighten one's apprehensions rather than allay them. Briefly put, the would-be saint need only wait for his mood to change to learn he is really a hypocrite. That is because true spiritual love is eternal, while the false is temporal, which means it is also temporary. The real thing lasts forever, whereas the hypocrites' Christian affections are "like a morning dew which is soon licked up by the sun . . . ; the heat of affections after other things licks it up."[26] Hypocrites may experience lavish amounts of "affection," analogous to a heavy dew, but "the love of Saints to Christ is like a spring," which may be "little" but never dries up. Shepard, who surely underwent manic-depressive personality swings, must have spent his life in constant anxiety, ever dreading the moment when the lavish affections he experienced in moments of religious exaltation would be licked up by the heats of other affections still lurking among the "turnings and deceits" of his heart.

As Shepard's modern editor, Michael McGiffert, observes, the brilliance of Shepard's analysis is most pronounced in his terrifying conception of the evangelical hypocrites—those "close deceivers of their own souls," as Shepard calls them. Such a person, McGiffert summarizes, "would be a zealous churchman and good citizen, have a choice character, display the insignia of grace, bear the name of Christian and sincerely believe himself to be 'wrapped up' in the Covenant; he would, in short, go the whole way to the Celestial Gates, trusting and humble—only to find the Gates shut against him." As Shepard's contemporaries recognized, this approach makes everyone liable, or even likely, to become a hypocrite. Still more disturbing is another of the "desperate consequences" of Shepard's theory explicated by McGiffert: "it made hypocritical one's perception of one's own hypocrisy and so destroyed the cognitive basis of assurance."[27]

The Parable of the Ten Virgins takes this sotereological Catch-22 still further, almost all the way to an unconscious admission that the victims of "hypocrisy of the heart" are in some sense unjustly condemned. Much of his comment on the supposed goodness of such hypocrites is obviously sarcastic: they are "such all-sufficient men, so good they need be no better, so wise that they need know no more." But the intention is not invariably satiric; sometimes Shepard seems close to pity: "And therefore consider of this, many a man hath been well brought up, and is of a sweet, loving Nature, mild, and gentle, and harmlesse, likes and loves the best things, and his meaning, and mind and heart is good, and hath more in heart than in shew, and so hopes all shall go well with him. I say, there may lie greatest hypocrisie under greatest affections; especially if they want light. You shall be hardened in your hypocrisie by them."[28] The trouble with this poor soul is not that he arrogantly confides in his own probity. He doesn't *pretend* to be decent, he *is* decent. In what, then, does his hypocrisy consist? It can only be in his *acting* just like one of the elect, when *in fact* he is not: his affections "want light." And so the more powerfully he experiences the affections, the more "hardened" a hypocrite he becomes. Such hypocrites don't necessarily think they are better than they are; their problem, rather, is that they're just not good enough and never will be. Self-deception allows them to be "good" people— but curing them of their self-deception would not be enough to remove the quotation marks from "good." On the contrary, were they to cease being self-deceived hypocrites they might find themselves compelled (by logic or fate) to become sincere, even earnest sinners.

Shepard's best attempt to crack the paradox probably comes in the chapter called "Containing a Discovery of Gospel-Hypocrites," in a section I have already referred to, where Shepard speculates that self-deceiving hypocrisy may be the biblical "unpardonable sin." He is speaking of persons who "beleeve, yet fail of saving Faith in regard of beleeving and closing with Christ." This latter part is the crux, for sometimes especially zealous hypocrites actually do "close with Christ, but 'tis without a high esteem of him, or love to him." There is that problematic word *love* again, and yet Shepard concedes that even of love perhaps "they have some, but right Grace consists in a kind of summity, or excellency, else 'tis not right." This process of infinite regression—from belief without faith, to faith without "closing," from "closing" without esteem and love, to love without "right Grace"—is probably a deliberate rhetorical strategy. Shepard is saying there is always something about a hypocrite that is *not* right, that just is not genuine and true. If it is not one thing, it is something else. His chilling and vivid illustrations perhaps make the point better than   11 the explanation: "As a man that lies on his death-bed, or in a Sea-storm in fear of Hell, he may now prize and take hold on Christ to save Him. A man lies upon the Bed of horror of heart, he may prize Christ to comfort him, and getting a conceit of it, be wrapt up almost in an extacy of joy, that a man would think he was sealed with the Spirit of Christ, and yet his end being naught, Christ only to comfort him, misseth of Christ in conclusion."[29] Our sympathy naturally goes out to such figures, and we account the perfectly human emotions they display as unpraiseworthy but hardly deserving of censure either. Yet Shepard, who knows how we feel and (more to the point) probably has a better than average imaginative grasp of how the characters in his examples would feel, is indeed insisting that they are hypocrites and their souls are thoroughly damnable.

By any standard, Shepard represents an extreme case. Even by Puritan standards he might be considered a victim of what some of them regarded as one of Satan's subtler ploys: attempting to drive a saint to despair by suggesting that his (accurate) intimations of election are merely further proof of his sinful presumptuousness. "To such as God doth Call, he doth reply,/That all their Grace is but Hypocrisy," as Edward Taylor versifies the devilish scam in *Gods Determinations touching his Elect*.[30] All the same I think it fair to argue that Shepard's case takes to an extreme nothing that wasn't there all along, implicitly or explicitly, in the Puritan mind, especially in New England. For American Puritans, it would appear, self-deceiving hypocrisy is an all but inescapable corollary of man's alienation from God. Just as only God can grant us saving faith, only God can free us from bad faith. Our own efforts either to win the former or repudiate the latter are equally unavailing.

For the Puritans, then, knowing whether you were a hypocrite was of vital importance in estimating your prospects for salvation. Moving from the individual to the community, knowing how many of the visible saints were hypocrites was a matter of vital importance with regard to national salvation. The idea of knowing the truth about the hidden self, whether applied individually or collectively, would seem well constituted to survive the waning of Puritan theological dominance of American religion and even the secularization of American culture generally. Jonathan Edwards, in attempting to revive the emotional spirituality of earlier Puritanism while reconciling it to Enlightenment rationality, jettisoned or at least poeticized much of the anthropomorphic literalness of his predecessors, and yet despite the influence of Lockean psychology on his thinking, his distinction between good and bad faith is of a piece with what we have seen from the previous century. Thus he interprets St. Paul's advice to congregants to "try themselves" as meaning that they should examine "their spiritual state and religious profession" in order to ascertain "whether they are disciples indeed, real and genuine Christians, or whether they are not false and hypocritical professors."[31] Even after the Calvinist revival fizzled, the idea of the self-deceiving, or "evangelical," hypocrite found secular uses in pre-Revolutionary agitation with reference to the sincerity of self-proclaimed patriots.[32] Perhaps this could be seen as an example of a phenomenon of current interest to students of American cultural history: the survival of certain words and the kinds of metaphors associated with them long after the Puritan theology from which they originated had lost its immediate relevance to American life.[33]

What makes it difficult to attribute the attitudes toward hypocrisy and self-deception held by Hawthorne (or by any writer of the New England Renaissance for that matter) to Puritan sources is the fact that very similar concerns are widespread in romanticism generally. For example, it would be impossible to disentangle Puritan and romantic strands in trying to account for the conflict that is pertinent to certain of Hawthorne's self-deceivers between their intellect and their emotions. "It is enough to understand," comments Norman S. Fiering, "that the seventeenth-century debates run smoothly into certain eighteenth-century issues and were part of the universal clashing motifs of 'heart' and 'head' in Western culture and in American literature in particular."[34] Unquestionably Hawthorne's fascination with hypocrites and self-deceivers should also be related to what has been called the "unmasking trend" in nineteenth-century European literature. Nevertheless, the similarities, which I hope will become apparent, between Hawthorne's characteristic approach in his fiction and that of the Puritans in their beliefs and practices to hypocrisy and self-deception are what gives a peculiarly American flavor to Hawthorne's contribution to "the systematic search for deception and self-deception and the uncovering of underlying truth," as the unmasking trend   13 has been described.[35] Even later in his career, when he no longer treats hypocrisy and self-deception as literary (if not literal) concomitants of damnation and instead attempts to incorporate the issues they raise into a broader exploration of the limits of art—even then the Puritan influence never entirely disappears.[36]

TWO

Tales and Sketches:
The Enigma behind the Mask

IN HIS BETTER WORK Hawthorne almost invariably reveals some unmistakable sign of a character's essential moral state at or near the end of a story, often at the moment of the character's death; furthermore, that final revelation almost always entails a recognition or at least an exposure of evil. The only important exceptions are all either children or virtuous women (usually virgins); their final revelations exhibit an inner wholesomeness that is metaphorically and sometimes all but literally angelic. But the palpable evil that resides to varying degrees in all the rest, after the hypocrisies and self-deceptions have been swept aside, is no doubt largely a product of Hawthorne's Puritan background, and as such it may come into conflict with his romanticism. His romantic trust in the spontaneous sincerity and goodness of the human heart remains at odds with his puritanical distrust of the heart's treachery, which human agency alone is inadequate to correct.

Let me try to illustrate how Hawthorne's residual Puritanism parts company with his romanticism by comparing his curious little sketch "Chippings with a Chisel" to an equally curious though more substantial prose work by Wordsworth on a similar sepulchral theme, the *Essays upon Epitaphs*. Wordsworth has two points to make, one artistic, the other philosophical. The more prominent artistic point is that insincerity is fatal to art while sincerity is absolutely necessary (although that does not mean that Wordsworth is opposed to conscious artistry in any form).[1] He proves this point empirically by assigning a more favorable critical evaluation to anonymous but original tombstone inscriptions than to formal epitaphs composed by established poets such as Pope. Wordsworth's other, more philosophical point, which is developed mainly by indirection, might be seen as the philosophical ground of the artistic point. Excellent original poetry arising from spontaneous emotions is possible because people are intrinsically good and so their spontaneous emotions are also good. Whatever comes directly from the heart is good and remains good unless externally perverted.[2]

In his sketch Hawthorne in effect accepts the artistic proposition but not the other. He actually outdoes Wordsworth (albeit partly in jest) with regard to the former by having it claimed that sincere mourners are able to turn out better sepulchral inscriptions than would an accomplished but unmoved poet even when they merely select a stock sentiment—"an ordinary verse of ill-matched rhymes, which had already been inscribed upon innumerable tombstones"—because somehow the profundity of their sorrow "makes the epitaph anew, though the self-same words may have served for a thousand years" (9:414).[3] Nonetheless, after overhearing such a selection being made by a "comely woman" on behalf of the deceased twin sister of her "pretty rose-bud of a daughter," Hawthorne as narrator raises with his alter ego the headstone carver (a fellow writer of sorts) the Wordsworthian objection that the mourning mother and sister should have tried to compose their own epitaph, for while he was listening to them he "was struck by at least a dozen simple and natural expressions from the lips of both." But the carver warns against "any new-fangled ones." His suspicion of romantic originality surely has much to do with his name, Wigglesworth, and with his being the "descendant of the old Puritan family." Yet this Wigglesworth is most unlike other Hawthornian Puritans and neo-Puritans in that he also embodies the romantic sensibility: we are told he possesses "a certain simplicity and singleness, both of heart and mind, which, methinks, is more rarely found among us Yankees than in any other community of people" (pp. 408–9). Wigglesworth the carver is in several respects an idealized version of Hawthorne the writer: a simplehearted man who is also a single-minded artist with a genius for putting into words the underlying truth of a person's life, which he knows (from his Puritan background) to be rarely what it seems to be on the surface.

16   He is an artist of the dead because in this sketch and elsewhere in

Hawthorne (most notably with Judge Pyncheon) a person's real self becomes manifest only in death. In life people may play various roles, but Wigglesworth sees to it that their tombs express the underlying truth, even when he is following their own testamentary instructions. Thus a "wretched miser" provides for himself "an immense slab of white marble, with a long epitaph in raised letters, the whole to be as magnificent as Mr. Wigglesworth's skill could make it," with the result that his miserly essence is immortalized by showing how "very characteristic" it was of him "to have his money's worth even from his own tomb-stone." This sham magnificence is instantly contrasted with the eloquent pathos of a moribund "poor maiden" who picks out "a slender slab . . . of a more spotless white than all the rest" on which to have her "virgin name" carved (p. 417). On one occasion the carver's success in revealing inner essences goes over the narrator's head, when he adds a cherub to the bow and arrows of the monument of an Indian chief. The narrator complains that the combination makes him think of Cupid, and the sculptor, "with the offended pride of art," answers with a wisecrack, neither denying the resemblance to Cupid nor bothering to point out the appropriateness of including a subtle hint of paganism in the grave of a converted heathen (p. 416). But on another occasion it is the narrator who interprets the deeper significance of the manner of interment, when a pair of bitter enemies are to be buried side by side. The carver supposes their dust will refuse to mix, but Hawthorne, relying on his own special talent for exposing the paradoxical qualities of emotions, disagrees, explaining to his simplehearted alter ego that what the two lifelong enemies "mistook for hatred was but love under a mask" (p. 415). The physiological fact of their putrefied remains mingling in the common grave directly symbolizes the hidden psychological truth of their lives.

In the grave there is only truth, with no room for lies. The village atheist wants a blasphemy on his stone, and Wigglesworth agrees to carve it because he has no doubt that whoever should read it would immediately apprehend as truthful the precise opposite of what the actual words were intended to denote, because "when the grave speaks such falsehoods, the soul of man will know the truth by its own horror" (p. 416). Presumably the sculptor means that the atheist's "avowal of his belief that the spirit within him would be extinguished like a flame" will be contradicted by his consignment 17 to the eternally flaming regions so graphically if ponderously described in the lumbering fourteeners of his ancestor, Michael Wigglesworth. Hawthorne, surely, doesn't intend us to think in such literal terms; nevertheless, he ends the sketch with a curious bit of dialogue that suggests his anxiety about revealing the soul's inner truth. The stone carver invites Hawthorne to choose a marker for himself, and the "somewhat startled" narrator replies: "To be quite sincere with you, I care little or nothing about a stone for my own grave, and am somewhat inclined to scepticism as to the propriety of erecting monuments at all" (pp. 417–18). He goes on to argue unconvincingly that graves interfere in some way with the spiritual side of being dead, a queer notion that the "good old sculptor" dismisses as nonsense or worse, and the question is left hanging. What the narrator really fears is having the sculptor do for him what he does for everyone else, which is to reveal one's hidden self through an inscription on a tombstone. Not only has the narrator learned by the end of the sketch just how incisive such revelations can be, but in a wider context there also lurks the understanding that Hawthorne practices the same craft in a different medium. In Hawthorne's literary equivalent to Wigglesworth's marble orchard, characters are immortalized not as they would like to think of themselves but as what they finally are, and for a sensitive man this is often a painful undertaking. More tenderhearted (if less simplehearted) than the thick-skinned Wigglesworth, Hawthorne questions the "propriety of erecting monuments at all."

In death our inner truth is laid open and fixed forever, but in life it remains concealed from others and even from ourselves, except in extraordinary moments of self-recognition. Even when the hypocrisy of society at large is painted with a broad stroke, as with the smug complacency of Father Hooper's parishioners or the "Christian" cruelty that pervades the world of "The Gentle Boy," it is clear that the unnamed multitudes would see themselves differently from how they appear on the page: the gap between what they seem and what they are is invisible to them. Only in "Young Goodman Brown" is there a vision of a community of *conscious* hypocrites, but the one who has the vision we are made to share is perhaps the greatest self-deceiver of all. In Hawthorne there is no sin, no guilt, no matter how flagrant or subtle, that can't be concealed to a certain degree (always with this qualification) from the guilty sinner's conscious apprehension until, like the inscription

Mr. Wigglesworth carves on a tombstone, it is set down forever by the art of fiction.

In the earlier Wigglesworth's *Day of Doom* the hypocrites play a prominent role, futilely proclaiming an integrity they lack, while divine justice unperturbedly combines their ranks with the less vociferous common reprobates, thus clearing the stage for the elect. Another Hawthorne sketch, "The Procession of Life," follows a similar pattern, and although more a "triumph" than an apocalypse, it is also a Wigglesworthian representation of doomsday in the sense that the good are set off from the wicked, and among the latter the hypocrites take center stage (in fact, they appear precisely in the middle of the sketch). But while the psychological condition of Wigglesworth's lost souls is not much gone into (they may be conscious hypocrites), the self-deception of the hypocrites in Hawthorne's procession could hardly have been made more explicit. "Here comes a murderer, with his clanking chains, and pairs himself—horrible to tell!—with as pure and upright a man, in all observable respects, as ever partook of the consecrated bread and wine. He is one of those, perchance the most hopeless of all sinners, who practise such an exemplary system of outward duties, that even a deadly crime may be hidden from their own sight and remembrance, under this unreal frost-work" (10:214). The murderer and his self-deceived spiritual brother are followed by a pair of floozies, who are similarly joined by a "decorous matron" and a "somewhat prudish maiden." What could they be doing here? the disingenuous narrator asks himself, and the sarcastic answer is: "We can only wonder how such respectable ladies should have responded to a summons that was not meant for them."

Hawthorne takes a paragraph to theorize on the psychological mechanisms that might explain such unlooked-for condemnations. The results are neither interesting nor instructive: Hawthorne's business, after all, is to show us these things, not account for them. "Statesmen, rulers, generals, and all men who act over an extensive sphere, are most liable to be deluded in this way," he proposes, because "they commit wrong, devastation, and murder, on so grand a scale, that it impresses them as speculative rather than actual." This is an obvious starting point for discussing some kinds of self-deception, but it would apply only to a comparative handful of cases and probably wouldn't be workable even for those. (Robin- 19 son's Hegelian analysis of Robert McNamara's behavior in the Vietnam era, for instance, begins from quite different premises.) What is of much greater importance in the paragraph is Hawthorne's offhanded assurance that, far from afflicting the high and mighty alone, or any limited group, sinful self-deception and hypocrisy may be the true condition of just about anyone: "But neither man nor woman, in whom good predominates, will smile or sneer, nor bid the Rogues' March be played, in derision of their array. Feeling within their breasts a shuddering sympathy, which at least gives token of the sin that might have been, they will thank God for any place in the grand procession of human existence, save among those most wretched ones. Many, however, will be astonished at the fatal impulse that drags them thitherward" (p. 215). They will be astonished to discover that they are really the opposite of what they believed they were. And yet, as we have seen in the case of the "evangelical" hypocrites of the Puritans, their striving after the good may merely compound their evil, which in the end is revealed: the fatal impulse drags them down. We feel "a shuddering sympathy," not only because there might go we, but also because we can't but feel that somehow those self-deceiving hypocrites are being held responsible for a situation created by something out of their control.

"Nothing is more remarkable than the various deceptions by which guilt conceals itself from the perpetrator's conscience," the paragraph continues. Equally remarkable are the profoundly human ways in which not only their guilt but their entire inner lives are concealed from the characters in Hawthorne's fiction until the moment of revelation, which often coincides with the moment of death. In taking up the shorter works, it should be understood that my aim is to be representative rather than comprehensive: so frequently are the themes of hypocrisy and self-deception encountered that to consider every instance would be tedious and repetitive. I hope to show how the methods or approaches established in the tales lead to Hawthorne's unsurpassed exploration of the themes in *The Scarlet Letter* as well as to their eventual subsumption into more purely artistic concerns in the later work.

I suggest that there are two distinct overall approaches to hypocrisy and self-deception in Hawthorne's fiction. One or the other may appear alone in a short work, though more often they function together. They correspond, roughly, to the moral and ontological dimensions of hypocrisy I discussed at the start of the last chapter.

The moral approach, the more obvious of the two, exploits inner/outer metaphors to suggest that our good, or true, selves lie within, and what is on the outside is not only literally but also morally external and false because it lacks (almost by definition) inner truth. Frequently this conception is expressed through images of masking or role-playing, as with traditional hypocrites, although Hawthorne's role-players are almost always self-deceivers as well, largely out of touch with the true selves within them and mistakenly placing their trust in what the reader recognizes to be a false outer appearance.

The other approach in a sense tends to subvert the first approach by raising the ontological question of what is real and what is not. Perhaps it can best be understood by an analogy with the theatrical mask. It has been observed of both ancient Greek drama and Japanese No plays that in the course of the performance the mask ceases to be a false appearance or disguise functioning as a counterfeit of the character but becomes a true realization of the character.[4] In an analogous manner, the figurative mask worn or role played by a Hawthorne character may also come to have or share in a kind of truth or reality.

Let me illustrate the two approaches with two very minor and comparatively simple stories. The first, "Mrs. Bullfrog," is in the long and inglorious tradition of wedding night jokes about the groom's letdown when at last he sees his bride as she really is. Hawthorne may well have had in mind this crude, sexist aspect of the tale when he wrote to Sophia: "As to Mrs. Bullfrog, I give her up to thy severest reprehension" (10:518). Bullfrog, the narrator, had wanted to possess the "most delicate and refined of women, with all the fresh dew-drops glittering on her virgin rosebud of a heart" (p. 136), and to all appearances that is what it seems he has got, until an overturned coach unmasks the true Mrs. Bullfrog: a bald, toothless brandy tippler with a nasty temper and lightning fists, who might not even be a virgin anymore—at any rate, a previous suitor had sacrificed everything he was worth to avoid keeping his promise to marry her. "You have ruined me, you blackguard!" she rages at the coachman who inadvertently unmasked her, perhaps with the same words she had used on the man who jilted her, "I shall never be the woman I have been!" (p. 132). 21

In any event, she has now become a real, flesh-and-blood woman for the first time, as opposed to the "young angel, just from Paradise" that Bullfrog has previously taken her for (p. 130). It is implied that he should bear some of the responsibility for his deception. "Women are not angels," his new wife enlightens him after she has had a chance to put her angelic appearance back on, and when he asks why women "conceal" their "imperfections," she calls him "unreasonable" and "strange," presumably for being so naive. On the one hand, the moral is simply that we should accept people despite their shortcomings. But at the same time, we learn at the end that Mrs. Bullfrog after all *is* an angel in a different sense: she will use the settlement awarded in her breach-of-promise suit to set her husband up in business. So the mask she wears of chastity and purity of heart, though it conceals a literally ugly truth, also embodies the spirtually beautiful truth of a woman giving everything she has to her man: "I have kept it all for my dear Bullfrog!" "The basis of matrimonial bliss is secure," exults "Happy Bullfrog" in the final paragraph, and he folds her to his heart. The antithesis of false exterior and true interior are, like the vehicle of the tale, effectively overturned.

Hawthorne has further sport with outer appearance and inner truth in another minor piece, "Feathertop," wherein a witch sets loose an animated scarecrow whose fine appearance wins instant acceptance in a society pervaded by hypocrisy and falsehood. Because in this society seeming to be other than what one is has already been established as a universal practice, "of all the throng that beheld him, not an individual appears to have possessed insight enough to detect the illusive character of the stranger, except [for obvious reasons] a little child and a cur-dog" (10:240). One of the leaders of this easily fooled society, a man who is "magistrate, member of the council, merchant, and elder of the church" (p. 233), suspects the devious purpose of Feathertop's mission because he too is secretly of the devil's company. The witch refers to this social pillar as a "snuffling hypocrite" (p. 245), and indeed he is one of Hawthorne's few fully intentional hypocrites. Everyone else, it would seem, except the child and the dog, falls for the trick because of self-deception, which always has moral overtones in Hawthorne, even in as silly a piece as this. Thus the magistrate's daughter can deceive herself into loving the scarecrow's semblance of a man just as easily as she earlier looks upon her full-length reflection as a true equivalent of her entire being. "In short," Hawthorne comments on her primping, "it was the fault of pretty Polly's ability, rather than her will, if she failed to be as complete an artifice as the illustrious Feathertop; and when she thus tampered with her own simplicity, the witch's phantom might well hope to win her" (p. 240). Polly is pretty without the "artifice," which only makes her "foolish" and might end in making her evil should she persist in her refusal to face the truth. Mirrors don't lie, particularly hers, which is "one of the truest plates in the world," and the girl is saved when she at last sees the truth in it, that she is a self-deceived girl in love with an absurdity.

Feathertop also sees himself for what he really is, but Hawthorne gives the problem another twist when he shows that the scarecrow has been self-deceived about his humanity. "The wretched simulacrum! We almost pity him. He threw up his arms, with an expression of despair, that went farther than any of his previous manifestations, towards vindicating his claims to be reckoned human. For perchance the only time, since this so often empty and deceptive life of mortals began its course, an Illusion had seen and fully recognized itself" (p. 244). Feathertop is now an undeceived self-deceiver, a state that the witch, speaking no doubt for the author (a fellow enchanter), declares to be anything but common: " 'There are thousands upon thousands of coxcombs and charlatans in the world, made up of just such a jumble of worn-out, forgotten, and good-for-nothing trash, as he was! Yet they live in fair repute, and never see themselves for what they are! And why should my poor puppet be the only one to know himself, and perish for it?' " (p. 245). As Newton Arvin observes, it is in this sense that Feathertop is "unique"—"because he catches sight . . . of his true and trashy self, and thereupon gives over the sorry pretence of grandeur."[5] But he is unique in precisely the opposite sense as well. Near the beginning of the tale, when the newly created "figure" calls the witch "kind mother" and promises to obey her "with all my heart," she almost splits her sides laughing as she takes his words literally: "With all thy heart! And thou didst put thy hand to the left side of thy waistcoat, as if thou really hadst one!" (p. 232). But at the end, *after* the creature has allowed its appearance to resume its original rags and straw, the witch reverses the earlier observation: "He seems to have too much heart to bustle for his own advantage, in such an empty and heartless world" (p. 246).

23

Compared to everyone else, Feathertop had an inner self that was true and noble: the rags and straw were the false appearance, and the handsome young man of the illusion paradoxically was all along his true inner substance. Even the mirror, after all, can only reflect with surface accuracy: it would show the hypocritical magistrate as an upright man, for instance, and not the emptiness and heartlessness of his wicked essence. In a hypocritical world, only an "Illusion" is capable of being true to his inner goodness.

In "Feathertop," the moral element is not insisted upon all that seriously; when it is, the complexity is magnified. Taking the tales as a whole, I have identified three different ways in which hypocrisy and self-deception produce evil consequences. These categories should be regarded more as a critical convenience than as a formal scheme for ordering Hawthorne's short fiction. First, there are stories about basically good people who, self-deceived as to their own interests and desires, try to avoid their proper places in life and act roles they are ill-suited to take on. The characters in the second group are closer to traditional hypocrites: their decent-on-the-surface lives conceal an inner evil from themselves and from others. The third category tells of those who are aware of their inner evil and may actually seek to confront it, which would seem to exempt them from the evils of self-deception at least, even should they lose all desire for virtue and become conscious hypocrites. Yet paradoxically, these last may ultimately become the greatest self-deceivers of all.

A straightforward example from the first group is "The Threefold Destiny," a story that strikes the modern taste as little more than clumsily contrived quasi-allegorical moralizing, although Hawthorne thought highly of it. It could also be classed with "The Ambitious Guest" and other stories in which a young man feels himself called to a life of memorable exploits when in fact his destiny is obscure. But whereas the nameless guest may indeed possess the qualities of a hero and would have succeeded were it not for the fateful avalanche, it is quickly established through a comic reversal that the protagonist of "The Threefold Destiny" did not in fact emerge from the romantic mold in which he fancies he was formed. He is introduced amid a wealth of exotic detail in keeping with the author's prefatory remark that the story belongs to an especially "fanciful," supposedly "eastern" genre. The protagonist, we are told, bears the outward marks of his globetrotting adventures, "exciting the gaze and curiosity of all" the passersby in his old hometown (and they probably don't even get to see one of the most atmospheric details provided to the reader: "the ataghan which he had once struck into the throat of a Turkish robber"). But his image is effectively punctured, for the reader if not for the townspeople, when a "young woman" is startled at the sight of him, but not in the way we might have expected, as the long descriptive paragraph is followed by a deflationary one-liner: "'Ralph Cranfield!' was the name that she half-articulated" (9:473). The name, of course, does it all: expecting Indiana Jones, we get Ralph Cranfield. His ever-faithful childhood sweetheart has recognized him for what he really is, and we soon learn that however much he may look the part, he is not at all comfortable with the swashbuckler role: "Alas! it was not with the aspect of a triumphant man, who had achieved a nobler destiny than all his fellows, but rather with the gloom of one struggling against peculiar and continual adversity, that he now passed homeward to his mother's cottage" (p. 475). He is a decent but unremarkable fellow who has been nearly broken as a consequence of his romantic self-deception, which we are led to believe had been produced or at least facilitated by enticing dreams.

The message, however, is not that he should have ignored the dreams or that he should look upon his vagabond years as wasted once he finally comes to appreciate the value of hearth and home. On the contrary, we again meet the paradox of the supposedly false outer appearance turning out to express the true inner essence after all, for when the local dignitaries come to offer him the schoolmaster's job, they neither want nor find ordinary Ralph Cranfield, and they behold instead "a tall, dark, stately man, of foreign aspect, courteous in demeanor and mild of speech, yet with an abstracted eye, which seemed often to snatch a glance at the invisible" (p. 477). The romantic image Hawthorne had ironically undercut at the beginning of the tale is reinstated, and this double reversal, as I see it, even serves to undercut the patent ironies with which the story concludes ("Instead of warlike command, or regal or religious sway, he was to rule over the village children!" and so on). He becomes the role he had originally deceived himself into assuming. A stranger would take him for a common school-teacher, but his students, presumably, would be aware that he is really a romantic adventurer.

A similar situation with an unhappy reversal produces sinister consequences in "The Shaker Bridal." Adam Colburn, like Ralph Cranfield, is marked out for a humble but happily married life, but he puts it off for the sake of vague ambitions: he "was loath to relinquish the advantages which a single man possesses for raising himself in the world." Unlike Cranfield, however, he gets no second chance, because "at no subsequent moment would matrimony have been so prudent a measure, as when they had first parted, in the opening bloom of life, to seek a better fortune." It is necessary to establish that the opportunity for marriage is gone forever (even though the reader has to suspend more than the usual quantity of disbelief to accept this) in order to drive home the tragedy of Adam's self-deception. He and Martha never have stopped loving each other ("they had held fast their mutual faith"), and both have turned down other, lucrative marriage offers (a clumsily inserted detail, meant to show that his aspirations for self-betterment weren't entirely grubby). In the absence of a compensating marital bliss, the failure of his ambitions to be satisfied affects Adam's mind with a "calm despair, which occurs only in a strong and somewhat stubborn character, and yields to no second spring of hope" (9:421–22), and in this mental condition he prevails on Martha to join the Shakers with him.

That Adam's problem has self-deception at its root can be seen when his conduct is compared to Martha's. When they are asked to accept leadership of the Shakers, thereby renouncing yet more irrevocably all prospects of a healthy relationship, Adam in effect claims he no longer loves his childhood sweetheart. "We are brother and sister; nor would I have it otherwise," he affirms. "And in this peaceful village I have found all that I hope for,—all that I desire," which couldn't be a flatter contradiction of all we know about him. Furthermore, the absolute certitude with which he says it—"My conscience is not doubtful in this matter"—demonstrates the depths of his dishonesty with himself. Martha, on the other hand, is dishonest with the others. About to endorse her lover's bad-faith declaration with an insincere speech of her own, she checks her words, fearful that "perhaps the old recollections, the long-repressed feelings of childhood, youth, and womanhood, might have gushed from her heart" (p. 423). So instead she tells a half-lie or at least deliberately conceals the truth as to her true sentiments. But unlike Adam, she can't conceal them from herself.

Though Adam bears much of the guilt for Martha's death, because we hold him responsible for her irrational and fruitless sacrifice to his idée fixe (reminiscent in this respect of Georgiana's sacrifice in "The Birth-mark"), at the same time we pity him because we understand he is self-deceived. Hence the irony of the final description of him, while she is expiring: "He, indeed, had withdrawn his hand from hers, and folded his arms with a sense of satisfied ambition" (p. 425). As opposed to the double reversal in Ralph Cranfield's fate—his childhood sweetheart *is* the mystery lady, the village school *is* a post of distinction—Adam gets only a cruel mockery of what he wanted: the woman he loves is dead, and the prominent position in society he coveted turns out to be pastoring a flock of emotional subhumans, people "who had overcome their natural sympathy with human frailties and affections" (p. 424). Yet he deceives himself into feeling satisfied. Only to the reader is his true miserable self revealed.

Adam's predecessor as leader of the Shakers, Father Ephraim, is more condemnable because he is more a hypocrite than a self-deceiver. Whereas Adam has successfully (and Martha unsuccessfully) repressed wholesome feelings, Father Ephraim before joining the Shakers "had been a dissolute libertine," so dissolute in fact that to purge himself it was necessary "to sear his heart of flesh with a red-hot iron" (p. 424). But in Hawthorne (as in Freud) repressed sexual impulses have a way of returning in some other form, and Father Ephraim's lascivious desires have come back as sadism and nihilistic despair. He chooses Adam and Martha to succeed him even though everyone knows they love each other. He wants them to live in misery; he wants the whole world to live in misery and die, leaving him the only conscious being, as he makes plain in his prayer to hasten the time "when children shall no more be born and die, and the last survivor of mortal race, some old and weary man like me, shall see the sun go down, never more to rise on a world of sin and sorrow!" Obviously, it is extirpating the world, and not ridding it of sin and sorrow, that excites Father Ephraim. Presumably he is to some extent a sincere convert to the misanthropic religion and therefore a self-deceiving hypocrite in that he persuades himself he is doing good. Nonetheless, we readily conclude from his words and actions that he is fundamentally evil, far more so than Adam. He is also more hypocritical in that his real reasons for prohibiting love in others is self-hatred for being incapable of love himself, and so in the name of a religion of love he more or less consciously defames love as nothing more than lust, which is all he has ever felt.

The title character in "Wakefield" also turns his back on humble domesticity. Here, however, his reasons for doing so are mysterious. Ralph Cranfield and Adam Colburn had lofty but conceivable roles cast for themselves, and both ironically came to fill them—with happy irony for the former and cruel irony for the latter. But Wakefield doesn't know what he wants or even what exactly he is doing when he leaves wife and home without a word and stays away for twenty years. Hawthorne doesn't seem to know what he is doing with the story, either: he refers to it as a "frolic, or whatever it may be termed" (9:133) and goes into his protagonist's motives no further than: "A morbid vanity . . . lies nearest the bottom of the affair" (p. 134). His main excuse for such vagueness is that Wakefield is "feeble-minded," but there is also a sense that the role he tries to play can hardly be put into words. The story begins with a two-paragraph preface asserting how fascinating and profound the whole idea is: "the incident, though of the purest originality, unexampled, and probably never to be repeated, is one, I think, which appeals to the general sympathies of mankind" (pp. 130–31). The story ends by calling Wakefield "as it were, the Outcast of the Universe," which seems grandiose to say the least, but I don't think we are meant to take it ironically and laugh, as if the story were a prose parody of Byron's *Cain.* Wakefield's identity is the central issue, and yet about all we ever learn is that he changes it—he even gets a red wig (p. 135)—but what he changes it to remains a mystery, most of all to himself, because we are also told he is a self-deceiver: "changed as he was, he would seldom be conscious of it, but deem himself the same man as ever." He believes he is still an ordinary man in a disguise, not realizing he has become the Outcast of the Universe. Which is to say, he (like Ralph and Adam) has truly become the role he assumed, even though he never becomes aware of it, except on rare occasions when "glimpses of the truth, indeed, would come, but only for the moment; and still he would keep saying—'I shall soon go back!'—nor reflect, that he had been saying so for twenty years" (p. 138).

Perhaps Hawthorne is uncommitted as to whether Wakefield's experience should be depicted as a silly escapade or a cosmic adventure because he can find no moral value to draw from the situation. As the moral issues grow more urgent, his tone grows darker.

The main issue in "Fancy's Show Box," stated in the introductory paragraph, is the relative moral status of "guilty thoughts" as compared to "guilty deeds" (9:220). Neal Frank Doubleday has traced the genesis of the sketch to a passage on the same issue in Jeremy Taylor's *Ductor Dubitantium*, a book which we know Hawthorne had seen previously and which he would later mention by name in another story, "Egotism; or, The Bosom Serpent."[6] Taylor was also concerned, though not quite so much as his Puritan contemporaries, with the problems of hypocrisy and self-deception, and I believe that some of his (and their) concerns are revived in Hawthorne's little "morality." A crucial matter in Taylor's book is how the conscience tells us when we are in a state of sin; he had no doubt that it always does so, if only we can read the message. Unfortunately, it is not always easy, inasmuch as there are "those sins where the Conscience affrights" and "those in which she affrights not," a distinction he illustrates by comparing clocks that strike the hour to clocks that do not strike. If a man is worried that his clock may be a nonstriker, he needs to pay closer attention to it, for "by this he may as surely see what the other hears, *viz.* that his hours pass away, and death hastens, and after death comes judgment."[7]

The message of Hawthorne's sketch may be that if you've neglected Taylor's timely advice and you've fallen into a complacent ignorance about your true moral state, you are lost unless your conscience finally begins to strike, and the louder the better. In the sketch, time has almost run out for aged Mr. Smith, a lifelong self-deceiver "who had long been regarded as a pattern of moral excellence" (p. 220). What keeps him from being totally evil and beyond redemption is that he is not entirely in agreement with the universally accepted opinion of his morally upright blissfulness. He feels "chill and sad" and doesn't know why until his conscience (accompanied by two other allegorized figures thrown in largely to make the scene more picturesque) comes to set him straight. "How kind," exclaims the narrator, for the abstract trio "to visit the old gentleman, just as he was beginning to imagine that the wine had neither so bright a sparkle, nor so excellent a flavor, as when himself and the liquor were less aged" (p. 221). How kind, that is to

29

say, for his conscience to apprise him of his long accumulated though hidden sins, so he might repent before it was too late.

Smith is given a last chance not because he has somehow earned it but rather because he is a good man at bottom and therefore has been providentially prevented from falling into the deeper sins to which the evil part of his nature might otherwise have led him. Some critics have misread the piece by concluding that Smith merely had an occasional wicked thought and nothing more, and they go on to lament Hawthorne's supposedly extremist moral standards.[8] But morality doesn't need to be stretched beyond the bounds of reasonableness to determine that Smith is far from being as righteous as he appears. True, his carnal appetites regarding his "first love" probably didn't come any closer to fulfillment than a wet dream (p. 222), but his attack on his "earliest and dearest friend," although not premeditated, was homicidal in intent: "Mr. Smith, in deadly wrath, had flung a bottle at Spencer's head" (pp. 223–24). Even in an earthly court he probably would have been convicted of voluntary manslaughter, possibly of a lesser degree of murder. But "it missed its aim"—note the pronouns: the *bottle* missed, not Smith, as if something external had saved the temporarily evil Smith from the consequences of accomplishing his momentary desire. Something similar intervenes to stop the last specified crime in the sketch, which is perhaps the gravest because it is contemplated by Smith not in the heat of youthful passion but cold-bloodedly in his maturity. The details aren't specified, but it is said to involve "devilish" legal robbery of no fewer than "three orphan children." Again, Smith is rescued from his own worse self: "Fortunately, before he was quite decided, his claims had turned out nearly as devoid of law, as justice" (p. 224). With the escape of all the others Smith remains the only victim of his wickedness: hence the self-conscious device in the sketch of his face in a mirror. For example, the bottle flung at Spencer "merely smashed a looking-glass" instead, and we don't need to be told whose reflection was in it at the time.

Smith is fortunate because, now that he has belatedly been pricked by conscience, he can set things right by repenting, for "there is reason to believe," as Hawthorne sermonizes, "that one truly penitential tear would have washed away each hateful picture, and left the canvas white as snow" (p. 225), like his repentant soul, we assume. But because his sins have been of the kind

Jeremy Taylor would have classed as nonaffrighting, he needed a dagger-wielding conscience to transform his vague malaise into an honest apprehension that his wholesome exterior conceals an inner rot that can be excised only by true repentance. The piece concludes that when a man "shall knock at the gate of Heaven, no semblance of an unspotted life can entitle him to entrance there" (p. 226). There is just no getting round that gate, as self-deceived hypocrites learn to their surprise.

The depiction of Smith's sins of lust, wrath, and greed are deliberately generalized for the same reason that he is given an Everyman-type name: to show not only that we are all guilty but also that we are all more or less self-deceived. Perhaps the most extreme example in Hawthorne of a story in which all of society is shot through with hypocrisy and self-deception is "The Gentle Boy." There are only two exceptions (the usual ones in Hawthorne): the innocent child who is the title character and Dorothy, a virtuous woman. Everyone else either is or becomes a hypocrite and self-deceiver, playing the role of Christian while actually embodying un-Christian, even anti-Christian impulses. The specific nature of these hidden impulses is not made plain, though I rather like Frederick C. Crews's idea that the Puritans are sadists and the Quakers are masochists, both made for each other.[9] What is important is that members of both groups are concealing something evil, and the reader quickly learns to estimate their true inner selves in terms opposite to the outer appearances they project. Thus Hawthorne, borrowing the sentiment from an actual historical document,[10] has a Puritan clergyman justify the oppression of Quakers by warning of "the danger of pity, in some cases a commendable and Christian virtue, but inapplicable to this pernicious sect." The narrator explicitly points up the hypocrisy of the man's now advocating what he once condemned: "In his younger days he had practically learned the meaning of persecution, from Archbishop Laud, and he was not now disposed to forget the lesson against which he had murmured then" (9:79–80). Meanwhile, the angelic purity of the accursed Quaker boy as he enters the Puritan meetinghouse is set off by the all but caricatured hypocrisy of the clergyman's parishioners:

> The wrinkled beldams involved themselves in their rusty cloaks
> as he passed by; even the mild-featured maidens seemed to

dread contamination; and many a stern old man arose, and turned his repulsive and unheavenly countenance upon the gentle boy, as if the sanctuary were polluted by his presence. He was a sweet infant of the skies, that had strayed away from his home, and all the inhabitants of this miserable world closed up their impure hearts against him, drew back their earth-soiled garments from his touch, and said, "We are holier than thou." (p. 79)

The miserable world's holier-than-thou inhabitants, of course, in their universal self-deception would be the last to suspect who is really polluting the temple.

The Quakers also involve themselves in hypocrisy. We are told of the boy's mother, Catharine, that "hatred and revenge" had "wrapped themselves in the garb of piety," which is further specified as a "shapeless robe of sackcloth" that is "girded about her waist with a knotted cord." This is the costume of a hypocrite if ever there was one, worthy of a fasting Pharisee: she even strews ashes on her head and displays a "deathly whiteness of a countenance . . . emaciated by want." Her hypocrisy is also brought out by the theatricality of the speeches she delivers, here as elsewhere in the tale,[11] calling down destruction in the name of religion. Curiously, she claims the Puritans have been deceived by the devil in disguise, and yet unlike the case with the Puritans, whose no doubt comparable psychological state we must infer, we are told almost in so many words that Catharine is self-deceived. Her "flood of malignity" is something "she mistook for inspiration" (p. 82), and she has experienced "happy visions, with which her excited fancy had often deceived her, in the solitude of the desert, or in prison" (pp. 83–84).

As always in Hawthorne, self-deception may extenuate but it never excuses sin. Compared to Dorothy, the child's virtuous foster mother, whose "very aspect proved that she was blameless, so far as mortal could be so, in respect to God and man," the boy's neglectful real mother, Catharine, "in her robe of sackcloth and girdle of knotted cord, has as evidently violated the duties of the present life and the future, by fixing her attention wholly on the latter" (p. 85). Hawthorne establishes her guilt yet more securely by granting her a moment in which the truth of the matter seems within her comprehension, though he adroitly avoids committing himself to saying just how thoroughly she ceases to be self-deceived. As she embraces the child she had given up for dead, we are told "it would seem that the indulgence of natural love had given her mind a momentary sense of its errors, and made her know how far she had strayed from duty" (p. 84). It doesn't last, though. Something similar occurs among the onlooking Puritans, who seem inclined to disregard their pastor's sermon and take pity on their fellow Christians. But for them the experience is barely even "momentary." Hearing Catharine moan "did not fail to move the sympathies of many who mistook their involuntary virtue for a sin" (p. 85), meaning that they fall back almost instantly into their habitual hypocrisy and self-deception, regarding virtue and sin as their opposites, and not really wanting virtue in the first place (it was "involuntary"), though they doubtless suppose they do.

The world of this story is especially depressing because there is no escape from deceitfulness. Of the two nonhypocrites, Dorothy survives but in joylessness, while in the end the innocent child is destroyed by the hypocrisy that surrounds him. Earlier he had been broken, in body and in spirit, when another boy he had selflessly befriended turned on him, in one of Hawthorne's most powerfully written sequences. Less violent but no less sad is the slow conversion—also described with consummate artistry[12]—of the foster father, Tobias, from being a Puritan with a good heart to being a Quaker hypocrite, his future personality prefigured by the nameless old Quaker who sits with him outside the child's death chamber. The old man got the call when his "dearest" daughter was dying, whereupon he "gat me gone." Tobias reasonably asks how a human being could do such a thing, and the old man admits that once he was "assailed by the thought that I had been an erring Christian, and a cruel parent," and he even had a vision of his daughter saying, "Father, you are deceived" (p. 98). But he managed to get over that moment of undeception so successfully that, when Catharine shows up just in time to learn she is about to lose her child, the old man offers his ghoulish congratulations: " 'Hitherto, Catharine, thou hast been as one journeying in a darksome and difficult path, and leading an infant by the hand; fain wouldst thou have looked heavenward continually, but still the cares of that little child have drawn thine eyes, and thy affections, to the earth. Sister! go on rejoicing, for his tottering footsteps shall impede thine own no more' " (p. 101). Provoked beyond even her voluminous capacity for self-deception—that is, unable to emulate the old man

33

in ignoring her anguish over the fate of her child—Catharine comes very close to cursing God. The end of the story proper has the child dying in her arms, though a short epilogue is tacked on to inform us that the king made the Puritans leave the Quakers alone, and Catharine went on to become a loved and valued member of the community. Both these appended developments would be meaningless in the deceitful world the story has so effectively exposed.

The world of "The Gentle Boy" is a vile place, not so much because its inhabitants are hypocrites and self-deceivers, but rather because their hypocrisy and self-deception are unforgivably evil, and the evil is inescapable. The dying boy apparently forgives his mother but we don't, although we may sympathize when she demands of the old Quaker, "What has God done to me? Hath He cast me down never to rise again? Hath He crushed my very heart in his hand?" (p. 102). But our sympathy for her is scant, not because we affirm the grim justice of her fate, but because in this story there seems to be no mercy—no other possible methods for the disposition of any human heart except by either crushing it or hardening it, as with the old Quaker's heart. Either they break or they petrify; they can't live. The gentle boy's dying words are: "I'm happy now" (p. 104), and it is difficult to take that unironically, although Hawthorne probably intends us to, or so the unconvincing epilogue would suggest.

A somewhat more positive, or at least more tolerant, response to a world of hypocrisy and self-deception is seamlessly integrated all through the text of "The Minister's Black Veil," in which we are consoled with the realistic assurance that, as Crews succinctly puts it, "the best approximation to happiness rests in an ignorant, busy involvement with a society of unconscious hypocrites." The only trouble with this formulation is that it neglects the other side of our reaction to the story, which includes a grudging admiration, or maybe it is more a horrified fascination, with Hooper's Alceste-like mission in quest of total sincerity. Crews sees Hooper in the "quintessentially Hawthornian situation" of being "a pathetically self-deluded idealist who, goaded into monomania by a certain incompleteness in his nature, ends by becoming the one obvious exemplar of the vice he rightly or wrongly attributes to everyone else."[13] Hooper's mistake, then, lies not in *being* a self-deceiving hypocrite but in worrying about it too much and thereby cheating himself of happiness.

34

In a short but well argued study of the tale, Nicholas Canaday, Jr., cleverly employs as a gloss on Hooper's character the following passage from Reinhold Niebuhr:

> If others will only accept what the self cannot quite accept, the self as deceiver is given an ally against the self as deceived. All efforts to impress our fellowmen, our vanity, our display of power or of goodness must, therefore, be regarded as revelations of the fact that sin increases the insecurity of the self by veiling its weakness with veils which may be torn aside. The self is afraid of being discovered in its nakedness behind these veils and of being recognized as the author of the veiling deceptions. Thus sin compounds the insecurity of nature with a fresh insecurity of spirit.[14]

On the basis of the Niebuhr passage, Canaday tries to show that Hooper is not merely misguided but actively wicked. His motives in taking the veil are "satanic, motivated by despair and pride. . . . With diabolical irony, he mocks himself and his God." He is self-deceived, but not about the possibility of avoiding deceit; instead, he deceives himself into believing he has "a new and superior perspective on human life" and that he has conquered his own nature: "At the moments when he smiles, Mr. Hooper is deceiving himself into believing that he has resolved the tension of his warring self." Yet some part of him remains aware of his true spiritual state, and Canaday interprets as a brief respite from his self-deception the incident at the wedding when he shudders at his reflection in a wine glass: "Essentially this is a moment when Mr. Hooper sees that he has redoubled his own sin, a moment of self-transcendence when he sees both the sinful nature of the act [of wearing the veil] and the results of it."[15]

Where this interpretation goes wrong is in taking Niebuhr's assertion that "the self is afraid of being discovered in its nakedness behind these veils and of being recognized as the author of the veiling deceptions" as a metaphorical description of Hooper's conduct, when actually it is more like a literal description. It is Hooper who is creating the metaphor; he is making a metaphorical statement out of his life. His metaphorical statement probably does have the same content as Niebuhr's, which is to say, both statements would mean more or less the same were they to be inter-   35 preted. But Hooper is not in the position of the veiled self of Niebuhr's sentence; he is, rather, in the position of Niebuhr, a theologian trying to shed light on the nature and destiny of man. It is, I agree, wrong of Hooper to throw away his happiness in order to make such a statement out of his life; however, the very wrongness of his so doing ultimately becomes a part of the statement his life makes.

As Michael J. Colacurcio has shown, Hawthorne set the story shortly before the outbreak of the Great Awakening of the 1740s to point up the contrast between the complacent, "backslidden" populace and the Puritan revivalists who would soon bring back temporarily the old fear and trembling. Alerting their congregations to the dangers of hypocrisy and self-deception was regarded as a crucial undertaking by the clergy of the Awakening, as it had been for their counterparts in the preceding century. Colacurcio may have identified a source for the story in an election sermon preached by William Cooper in 1740. Cooper's conviction that God "can't be deceived and will not be mocked" and that he "looks into the heart, and sees through all disguises" could well be taken for the text of the fictional sermon Hooper delivers; in any event, as Colacurcio comments, Cooper's "theme is, quite simply, the rationale of Hooper's ministry."[16] Hooper is a walking sermon, and his intention is to remind us of Thomas Shepard's gloomy discovery that anyone can be a sinful hypocrite and not know it because of self-deception. But there is another part of Hooper's message which Hooper did not himself anticipate, which is that ultimately it does no good to follow Shepard's example and spend your life worrying about whether you're an unconscious hypocrite, and it does no good trying to incite other people to worrying about whether they are. They won't listen for long and they won't understand. Another clergyman attempts to persuade the dying Hooper to remove the veil by asking, "Is it fitting that a father in the church should leave a shadow on his memory, that may seem to blacken a life so pure?" (9:51). The question shows that the clergyman (and therefore everyone else) has completely missed Hooper's point, which has been the same from the beginning: there is no such thing as a certifiedly pure life. Hooper takes one last stab at explaining by saying he sees a black veil (like his) on all their faces, but he only succeeds in frightening them away again. That is all he has ever succeeded in doing.

If Hooper has deceived himself, it is in this sense: he expects too much from his exemplary soul-searching as a means of inspiring his parishioners to search theirs. Like Thomas Shepard, he yearns for a self-knowledge that is beyond human attainment. Most people are best left to their humdrum everyday complacency and hypocrisy: they are sinful but not irredeemable. Hooper's mission is theologically quixotic, but his faith, at least, is genuine. Like Wigglesworth the tombstone carver, he believes that death reveals people for what they really are, and to that revelation he looks forward hopefully, though not smugly or complacently. "There is an hour to come," he tells his fiancée, Elizabeth, "when all of us shall cast aside our veils" (p. 46). He loses the opportunity for intimacy on earth with the woman he loves, but he really believes their posthumous existence together will more than make up for it: "Be mine, and hereafter there shall be no veil over my face, no darkness between our souls! It is but a mortal veil—it is not for eternity!" (p. 47). Understandably, the realistic Elizabeth, another of Hawthorne's virtuous virgins, isn't interested in marriage on those terms, but she remains faithful to him, thereby tacitly accepting, if not approving of his taking the veil.

The veil is to be removed after death within the sight of God; until then, it comes to represent Hooper's life. He gives his life to it. The veil is described as "hanging down from his forehead to his mouth, and slightly stirring with his breath" (p. 45), and again, when he is dying, it is seen as "reaching down over his face, so that each more difficult gasp of his faint breath caused it to stir" (p. 50). It will cease to stir, of course, when his breath, his spirit, has left him for good. Identifying his life with the veil implies that he is giving his life to death, but not in the sense that the old Quaker in "The Gentle Boy" or the retiring community leader in "The Shaker Bridal" give their lives to death. These two turn *against* life, whereas Hooper merely turns *away* from life, which is what makes him such an effective and cherished consoler of the dying (p. 49), who must do the same. An affinity with death is a constant feature of his character: even before taking the veil, his "customary walk" was to the graveyard at sunset (p. 48). But that doesn't mean he is morbid. Helping people on their journeys to the graveyard is the way he conceives of his calling, and it is a legitimate and respectable way, though Hawthorne and most of his readers could probably think of other ways that are better. Nonetheless, we are meant to sympathize with the humble, decent manner in which Father Hooper pursues his way, until "he had one congregation in the church, and a more crowded one in the church-yard; and having wrought so late into the evening, and done his work so well, it was now good Father Hooper's turn to rest" (p. 50). I detect no irony in this simple assessment of a long and devoted lifetime of service.

What makes Father Hooper good may also be, in addition to how well he does his job, his more than average blamelessness. Pressed by Elizabeth to explain why he covers his face, he won't even be specific enough to say whether it is for "secret sin" or for "sorrow" (p. 46). Perhaps he has really experienced neither: in terms of Puritan theology, he may be among those genuine elect who are tempted by the devil into suffering needless anxiety, so that his repentance, while valid in itself in view of the human condition generally, is superflous for him personally. If he is not quite blameless, there is still nothing to suggest he deserves for his sins the penitential suffering he embraces. That even a clergyman's costume can disguise a hypocritical sinner is part of his message; that a man who conceals his face from the world may actually have much less to hide than those who don't may be Hawthorne's, and his message to some degree subverts Hooper's puritanical over-emphasis of inner evil and overinsistence on unrelenting contrition. Yet his excessive guilt and sorrow, although misplaced, are not reprehensible morally. Hawthorne's most utterly lost souls are not those who suffer excessively but, quite the contrary, those whose capacity to experience guilt and sorrow is lacking or has been perverted. There are several such characters, and they all are hypocrites, self-deceivers, or both.

Gervayse Hastings in "The Christmas Banquet" is so transparently two-faced that he tries to deceive no one, least of all himself. Yet all others deceive themselves about him. On the outside he is prosperous enough to exceed "magnificence," virtuous in his "munificent liberality to the distressed," and provided with "domestic happiness" in the form of a charming family (10: 299–300). Yet in reality, despite his wealth he has a meager existence, his virtuous acts do not bring their own reward for him, and he becomes a stranger in his family. He is not an active wrongdoer, but his life is empty. Indeed, he might even commit wicked deeds if he thought they would allow him to feel guilty or sorry, but the capacity for such feelings is just what he lacks. This story is one of several in which Hawthorne brings in his heart-as-cavern analogy, and Hastings is described as *not* being one of "those whose hearts are cavern-mouths, through which they descend into a region of illimitable wo" (p. 296). Lacking the region of illimitable woe, he can't have the region of sunshine and flowers that lies beyond it in Hawthorne's notebook passage where the allegory first appears (8:237). Naturally, it is best to reach the sunshine even if it means passing through the illimitable woe, but, one is better off with only the woe, if the alternative is an existence with neither woe nor sunshine. There is nothing worse than that.

To make this point, Hawthorne contrasts Hastings's condition with every variety of sin and sorrow he can squeeze into one short story. The vehicle is an annual Christmas banquet for the wretched that is more like a blasphemous last supper, attended by twelve miserable, sinful creatures (counting the two stewards) and presided over by the veiled skeleton of a misanthropic atheist. As one would expect, the company always includes some choice hypocrites and self-deceivers—a "self-deluding fool" who believes he is called to a high destiny (p. 288), "a man of nice conscience" who killed someone but "could not absolutely determine whether his will had entered in the deed, or not" (p. 294), an unconscious Mammon-worshiper who "had been greatly perplexed at his invitation" because "he had no conception how miserable he was" (p. 295)—but they all agree that Hastings is above them with respect to deceitfulness: "The traitor!" they collectively mutter to themselves, "the vile imposter!" (p. 293), as they refuse to acknowledge his right to attend the banquet. In a neat switch they think he is a hypocrite because he claims to be the most miserable among them when he looks so happy, whereas in reality he is a hypocrite for the opposite reason, that he looks happy when actually he is the most miserable. But Hastings doesn't really want to deceive: the lie he seems to be telling (his misery) is really the truth, but no one will believe it. At the final banquet scene—comically loaded with extra dolor by adding a "side-table" for "three of four disappointed office-seekers," one of them perhaps representing Hawthorne himself—Hastings, like Father Hooper, makes a last effort to explain the meaning of his life, and his failure to get through to anyone is cleverly brought out by the comment of a frame story character who purportedly has been listening to the same fiction we have been reading. "It is true, I have an idea of the   39 character you endeavor to describe," she tells the frame story author, "but it is rather by dint of my own thought than your expression" (p. 305). I think she is speaking for Hawthorne, not just as a self-critic of his writing, but more profoundly in the sense that human life without guilt and suffering is inconceivable except as an abstraction. No wonder Gervayse Hastings is not what he appears to be: beneath the expressiveness of description he is only a bloodless idea.

If Hastings deceives himself, he does so by hoping against his own conviction of the futility of it that he may somehow be provided with a capacity for feeling, and at the final banquet he is still seeking among the guests for someone "who might impart to him the mystery—the deep, warm secret—the life within the life . . . whether manifested in joy or sorrow" (p. 301). He knows all too well why he is lost, but he cannot quite bring himself to accept that there is not a thing in the world he can do about it. The situation of the title character in "Ethan Brand" is in this respect almost the reverse. He, too, is aware of the critical state of his soul, having deliberately set out to commit wicked deeds, but he won't accept the fact that something always can be done about it: no sinner, however loathsome his crime, is beyond the compass of mercy while he lives. Nina Baym, drawing on the findings of others, concludes that the unpardonable sin Ethan Brand searches for is not any particular crime he committed, but, ironically, his own willful refusal to repent.[17] More recently, Baym has further argued that the emphasis of the story is psychological, not theological, and that Brand's problem boils down to an extreme case of monomania.[18] But there is no need to separate theology from psychology categorically. Brand's refusal to repent is damnable because it constitutes a denial of God's saving power and a hatred of God's grace; Brand, however, arrives at his refusal to repent through psychological means—by deceiving himself into believing he is already beyond redemption, when in fact he is not.

There is no need to embroil ourselves in a debate about what the unpardonable sin is supposed to be, although I'd like to point out, as Leonard J. Fick has already observed,[19] that Christ's statement concerning the unforgivability of "blasphemy against the Holy Ghost" comes in the context of another dressing-down of the hypocritical scribes and Pharisees: "O generation of vipers, how can ye, being evil, speak good things?" (Matthew 12:31, 34).

Though discussing a different text (Hebrews 10:29), Thomas Shepard in *The Parable of the Ten Virgins* similarly associates the unpardonable sin with the self-deceiving machinations of his "gospel hypocrites."[20] Publicly proclaiming his wickedness, Brand is not a hypocrite. But he deceives himself as to the magnitude of his sins. He proudly believes there is not a spark of good left in him, that his evil is of cosmic proportions, and yet everyone recognizes that he is just another snake of the common garden variety, "a sinner, like the rest of us," as his successor at the lime kiln puts it (11:90). Even though we are assured he has radically changed from what he was before leaving on his quest for perdition, nevertheless the prominence given a passage near the end of the story, describing his youthful nature, when he was "a simple and loving man" with "love and sympathy for mankind" and "pity for human guilt and woe," is probably meant to suggest that just enough goodness remains to him so that his damnation isn't quite the triumph over omnipotence one might be led to suppose from his grandiloquently satanic ravings. Like Ralph Cranfield, Brand has an inflated conception of his destiny; only in his case it is an evil destiny that his grandiose dreams delude him into pursuing.

His biggest crime does sound rather metaphysical: he may have "annihilated" a girl's soul (p. 94). But the girl, old Humphrey's daughter Esther, is also flesh and blood, and whatever it is Brand did to her soul, so far as we are told, the rest of her seems to have stayed in one piece. (My guess is that the girl's image is what startles Brand when he peers into the Jew's magic lantern: Brand is promised by the Jew, who knows him, that he will see "somewhat that is very fine," while shortly before we had learned that "fine stories" of the girl's circus appearances had been drifting back to the village.) We already noted the new lime man's assurance that everyone else in the story is as big a sinner as Brand, except presumably for the usual innocent child. That they are also mostly hypocrites of one sort or another may be indicated symbolically by having everyone put on a circuslike act or performance, as Roy R. Male has observed.[21] Oddly, Male exempts Brand from the program of circus attractions, although his daredevil performance on the high wire of sin and damnation promises to be the most flamboyant act of all. But challenging God is as futile and inane a pastime for a man as chasing its own tail is for a dog. In the end, Brand is dead and the sun rises so majestically that "it seemed   41 almost as if a mortal man might thus ascend into the heavenly regions" (p. 101). Any mortal man might have thus ascended, even Ethan Brand, if only he'd seen through his self-deception and repented.

A related self-deception similarly destroys the integrity of the title character in "Young Goodman Brown." Brand believes his sins are beyond forgiveness, while Brown thinks there is no forgiveness for anyone. The communion of the wicked that Brown beholds in the forest also resembles the sinners' march in "The Procession of Life," with hardened reprobates, "wretches given over to all mean and filthy vice," and accomplished hypocrites, "grave, reputable, and pious people," mixed together indiscriminantly: "It was strange to see, that the good shrank not from the wicked, nor were the sinners abashed by the saints" (10:85). Unlike "The Procession of Life," however, in Brown's vision there is no corresponding march of the genuinely good people. This is Satan's apocalypse that he witnesses, and yet it is really a concealment of truth and not a revelation. "Depending upon one another's hearts, ye had still hoped, that virtue were not all a dream. Now ye are undeceived!" preaches the devil at the climax of his sermon. But liar and father of lies that he is, what he says next, in the guise of undeceiving us, is in truth the greatest deception of all: "Evil is the nature of mankind" (p. 88).

As in all first-class lies, there is just enough truth in the devil's statement to make it compelling, just as there is enough hypocrisy and self-deception in the world to make credible Brown's exaggerated view of his fellow beings as he comes to see them in the forest. Before he could see nothing but good in other people, and now he can see nothing but evil: the shortness of the distance between the two extremes of misperception is a psychological fact which the devil exploits to win Brown's soul and which Hawthorne relies on to render Brown's turnabout in character plausible. Much less essential are the means by which the devil sets his snare: that is to say, it is not important to clarify the nature of what Brown thinks he sees—dream, hallucination, projection, etc.—so long as it is accepted that his vision does not yield the whole truth. My endorsement goes to the "spectral evidence" thesis put forward by Doubleday and others, which holds that the devil, who is to some degree a potentiality within Brown himself, employs phantoms in the semblance of real people,[22] "all whom ye have reverenced from youth. Ye deemed them holier than yourselves. . . . Yet, here are they all" (p. 87).

Whether they are really there is unimportant compared to the reasonable assumption that just about any of them *could* be there. That they could is the grain of truth in the devil's assertion that human nature is absolutely evil, a lying distortion of the human condition, which contains both a potential for evil and a hope of redemption. But Brown naively believes that some people are intrinsically holier than others and that there are living saints whose purity is above question. His wife, for instance, he refers to as "a blessed angel on earth" (p. 75), his father and his father's father never once strayed (pp. 76–77), and so on. Goody Cloyse calls him a "silly fellow" (p. 79), the word *silly* bringing in connotations of innocence on the one hand (compare German *selig*) and stupidity on the other. There is good reason to rely on the goody's terse assessment of Brown's simplemindedness; having taught him his catechism when he was a child (a role she continues to fill for the village children), now that he is a grown man she still functions as "his moral and spiritual adviser" (p. 78).

Were Brown intelligent enough to have been a theologian he might well have been among those who would demand that the visible church be purged of all sinners, secret or otherwise, and made perfect. It just might be relevant that the English Separatists, or Brownists, were sometimes accused by Puritan controversialists of Donatism,[23] although in historical fact their leader, Robert Browne, held that "there must needs be hypocrites in every church, & sometimes also open breach of God's commandments."[24] Goodman Brown is freed by the devil from his childish illusions of human sanctity, but instead of attaining a mature, balanced view he falls into equally lopsided delusions of human perfidy.

But Brown is not entirely innocent to begin with, as most critics have recognized. Commenting on Brown's profession of incredulity when the devil informs him of his ancestors' ruthless oppression of Quakers and Indians, Robert H. Fossum remarks that Brown must be an ironist, a hypocrite or an outstanding ignoramus. What Fossum finally decides upon would make of Brown something like what we have called a self-deceiving hypocrite: "Brown is not a conscious hypocrite; he has simply repressed his own secret sins along with any suspicions he may have of others."[25] I would qualify this by pointing out that, as is always the case with self-deception, these secret sins are not so "simply" repressed. Were he not conscious of his attraction to evil, he would not have gone to the forest in the first place. As he resolves, on leaving town, to cling to Faith in future, we are told that he "felt himself justified in making more haste on his present evil purpose" (p. 75). Clearly, the words "evil purpose" are given virtually as indirect discourse: he knows what he is up to. The same goes for "justified": this man has succeeded in convincing himself he can justly seek out evil. In other words, instead of openly acknowledging his capacity for evil and struggling with it, he hypocritically pretends he can save himself by hiding his wickedness behind what he supposes to be the irreproachable sanctity of his wife: "after this one night, I'll cling to her skirts and follow her to Heaven." It all comes down to a refusal to accept his own humanity or anyone else's. He should realize that, far from being an angelic visitor who can write his ticket to heaven, Faith is a woman who can be tempted. He should realize this because she tells him so: "A lone woman is troubled with such dreams and such thoughts, that she's afeard of herself, sometimes" (p. 74).

Again, it is not important how "real" is her presence in the forest (or, for that matter, the presence of her provocative pink ribbon). One argument against the spectral evidence explanation and in favor of her voluntarily being there is the psychological plausibility of her (perhaps momentary) reluctance to proceed at the point when Brown hears her voice in the darkness "uttering lamentations, yet with an uncertain sorrow, and entreating for some favor, which, perhaps, it would grieve her to obtain" (p. 82). After all, she already told him in effect that she might be tempted if he left her alone, and her simultaneous hunger for and revulsion from "some favor" is more compatible with a continued moral struggle on her part than with her being a mere phantom sent to delude Brown. Her struggle carries no weight with him in any case: he gives up on her and on the remainder of the human race as well. Nor is it worth the bother of speculating whether she looks up to heaven with Brown at the last moment. There is no last moment so long as life lasts, but Brown is buried with "no hopeful verse upon his tombstone" (p. 90) because he has long denied all hope. Brown sees in the human race as a whole what Ethan Brand sees in himself: no redemption. In this they have deceived themselves, to their despair.

The hypocrisy and self-deception practiced by individual characters and by the population as a whole in Hawthorne's short fiction always cause harm to themselves and usually bring evil to others as well. Sometimes his characters learn the truth about themselves and are thus granted an opportunity to live, or to die, honestly although painfully. At other times only to the reader is the truth revealed by a sign or symbol, and the hypocrite continues in (or dies in) self-deception, perhaps unaware even of the depths of his own misery, as is certainly the case with the new Shaker elder and probably also with Ethan Brand and Goodman Brown, who die unhappily but not knowing as we do that their very despair is their greatest delusion.

Considered ontologically, rather than morally, the issues are more complex. Except for the innocent child, the virtuous woman, and the odd cur dog, virtually all Hawthorne's characters wear a mask and play a role of some sort or other. But the masks they wear and the roles they play in some sense function with as much validity as expressions of their true selves as they serve to disguise some hidden, inner truth. This is clearest with the literal mask worn by Father Hooper: the minister's black veil becomes a vital part of his ministry. The outer appearance represented by the veil and the inner reality of the unseen face are inseparable at the moment of death when the truth is revealed, and the truth that is revealed itself wears a mask. The implication is that self-deception is possible, indeed all but inescapable, because the truth about the human self or soul is essentially and intrinsically unknowable, except by signs . . . a veil, the empty outline of a heart, a gravestone without a hopeful verse.

THREE

The Scarlet Letter:
A World of Hypocrites

I N *The Scarlet Letter*, as elsewhere in his fiction, and here as much as anywhere, we are in a world pervaded by hypocrisy and self-deception all but totally unrelieved, with no gentle boy to remind us that a translucent sincerity is at least still conceivable. The absence of unqualifiable genuineness contributes much to the novel's famous gloom; curiously, though, it also serves to lighten the dark onus Hawthorne usually places on the hypocritical populace as a whole, because in this story there are no gems for them to act as foils to. That is not to imply that he accepts hypocrisy or condones bad faith; rather, he pessimistically, if not cynically, resigns himself to their persistence. As a consequence, while the people at large are as great a collection of hypocrites as anywhere, here their hypocrisy is comparatively innocuous and is not so vigorously condemned. For example, when the same crowd of Puritan brats that ruthlessly trounce the gentle boy turn on Pearl, they do little harm and instead catch the worst of it, not only because Pearl is not gentle (although she does become a gentle-woman at the end), but also because Puritan hypocrisy simply isn't as pernicious here as it is everywhere else in Hawthorne's fiction. No Colonel Pyncheon falsely accuses a sorcerer in order to confiscate his property: the only witch who will be executed, Mistress Hibbins, really is a witch, or at any rate she thinks she is. Everyone is a hypocrite of one sort or other, but no one is a pernicious hypocrite except Chillingworth, and even he—unlike, say, Judge Pyncheon—is allowed some claim to justice and even a shred of hope for redemption: he is not an utterly damned hypocrite like the Judge. No one in this book is.

By overstating the degree to which Puritan hypocrisy is condemned in *The Scarlet Letter*, Allen Austin, in his marvelously concise essay on the function of satire in the book, correspondingly underestimates the extent to which hypocrisy is almost an expected part of life: we expect to encounter it throughout Puritan society, and we do. Austin claims that only the "elite" are hypocritical, and while he marshalls in brief scope the most telling instances of upper class hypocrisy—the wealthy Puritans who profess spirituality and disdain for ornament but reveal their love of money and their ostentation through buying Hester's fancywork and hoping to marry their sons to the once-despised Pearl after she inherits Chillingworth's fortune, and so on—he offers little in defense of his counterthesis, that the "common people" are not hypocritical.[1] Yet there is sufficient reason to conclude that they are hypocrites too. It is true, as Austin points out, that we are told Hester would have received more "sympathy" from the "larger and warmer heart of the multitude" than from the rulers; nonetheless, the occasional close-ups we get of the multitude suggest an equivalent capacity for hypocrisy and perhaps an even greater sense of vindictiveness than we find in their betters. After all, the establishment had decreed a relatively mild punishment for Hester's capital crime, for which, moreover, the culprit refused to name her accomplice and showed no remorse. The female representatives of the common people who await Hester's emergence from the prison, on the other hand, reject their leaders' restraint. Not only are these beefy, broad-shouldered "matrons" without compassion, but they are hypocrites in that their indignation over the mildness of Hester's punishment is motivated not by respect for "the Scripture and the statute-book," as they claim, but by envy of Hester's feminine good looks. One, "a hard-featured dame of fifty," insinuates (probably with accuracy) that "the hussy" got off so lightly because her judges were men, whereas "we women" would have been harsher. Another, described as "autumnal," wants to have "the naughty baggage" branded on the forehead, while the one who calls for hanging is "the ugliest as well as the most pitiless"—in this case they clearly go together. Presumably the "young wife" who tries to put in a word edgewise for the quality of mercy, without anyone   47 paying attention, is better looking; in any event she doesn't live very long, unlike the female hypocrites, who seem healthy enough to go on forever (pp. 51–52). Other common people exhibit similar characteristics. The elite may be hypocritical in creating a market for Hester's finery, but at least they pay for it, as opposed to the "poor," who accept handouts from her, even though they are "less miserable than herself," whereupon they return "a gibe in requital," as if they, no less than the formally recognized saints, were too good to consort with a formally recognized sinner (pp. 84, 83, 161). Perhaps Hawthorne's repeated praise of the multitude's warmheartedness should be taken as mere platitudes, if not as intended ironies. It is difficult to imagine from what we actually see in the novel concerning the common people, as opposed to what we are told, that the world's "great heart" really would have "pitied and forgiven" Dimmesdale had he been more forthcoming sooner (p. 139). (It is possible also that such assertions are calculated to increase the pathos of Dimmesdale's position by suggesting that his paralyzing fears were after all groundless.) Of course, not all the false behavior attributed to average people is so insidious; probably most of it is petty and more or less harmless, such as the self-deception of the "virgins" in Dimmesdale's congregation, who "imagined" their devotion to their pastor "to be all religion" (p. 142). But aside from outsiders like the Indians and the sailors, no one is completely clear of hypocrisy and self-deception, and for that reason, in part, less mischief arises that is directly attributable to those phenomena, outside the central situation, than we find in other stories. Their very ubiquity lessens their harmfulness.

So ubiquitous are they that even some of the major symbols in the novel are affected. I don't mean to raise the banal semitautology that the symbols are ambiguous; nor do I intend belatedly to launch an expedition into the dark continent of Hawthornian symbolism, an undeniably important realm in his total achievement but one that is largely tangential to my present concerns. What I mean is that some of the symbols seem virtually designed to be deceptive in that they purportedly represent something other than what they actually represent. The central symbol, the letter *A*, generally speaking does not belong in this category because, although it may be the initial letter of many words, some of which would conflict with each other, it is never said, not even indirectly, to stand for anything at all, and in the end it comes to stand simply for itself. One, at least, of its particular manifestations does, however, function deceptively: the meteoric *A* Dimmesdale and others imagine they see in the sky. Dimmesdale connects the apparition to his guilt, and the narrator concurs so far in this interpretation as to qualify it by commenting that "another's guilt might have seen another symbol in it" (p. 155). The sexton of Dimmesdale's church, on the other hand, says that "we" interpret it as standing for "Angel," in commemoration of Governor Winthrop's death and as a sign, presumably, of his salvation (p. 158). Like a hypocrite, the meteor shows an angelic face to the world and a diabolic face to the inner eye. Furthermore, the very light it casts is deceptive, illuminating the scene "with the distinctness of mid-day" but maintaining the concealment of the night, so that instead of "the light that is to reveal all secrets," it becomes a light that strangely hides the truth. No one from the community sees the truth revealed on the scaffold, while Dimmesdale, looking back at Chillingworth, evidently fails to appreciate what he "appeared to see": the truth about the devilish hypocrisy of Chillingworth, who might "have passed with them for the arch-fiend, standing there, with a smile and scowl" (p. 156). As Fogle sums up, in the context of relating the incident to Hawthorne's well-known Coleridgean theory of the imagination, "the meteor itself suggests both transcience and possible deceit."[2]

Possible deceit is suggested by another, more important symbol: flowers, particularly roses. Next to the symbols related to the letter, the flower symbols are probably the most meaningful in the book. They emphasize the universality of the story: A. Robert Lee has recently observed that because the rosebush beside the prison is said to still be alive it constitutes a symbolic bridge between the Puritan world and ours.[3] Another indication of the centrality of the rosebush is the bold manner with which Hawthorne explicitly identifies it with the book itself: "Finding it so directly on the threshold of our narrative, which is now about to issue from that inauspicious portal, we could hardly do otherwise than pluck one of its flowers and present it to the reader" (p. 48). The "inauspicious portal" is figuratively the beginning of the book, while literally it is the prison door from which Hester and the infant Pearl, the initial subjects of the narrative, are about to appear—or are about to be "plucked" and presented to the reader. Hester and Pearl, then, are associated with the rosebush from the outset.

The problem is that the prison, which at that moment literally houses (threshold, portal and all) the future subjects of the narrative, is also called a flower: "the black flower of civilized society" (p. 48). Like the prison and the rosebush, black flowers and red flowers (or wildflowers) are closely associated, and their references are blurred and mingled to such a degree that they cannot be neatly distinguished, not even in moral terms. In his remarks on the vegetation imagery, Waggoner concludes that "Chillingworth is associated with weeds, Pearl with flowers, and Dimmesdale with no natural growing thing at all," and "Hester walks her ambiguous way between burdock and rose."[4] However, Chillingworth also gathers, besides medicinal roots and weeds, "the blossoms of wildflowers" (p. 121), and he later says of his obsessive lust for vengeance: "Let the black flower blossom as it may" (p. 174). Canaday proposes that the rose symbolism comes from Dante and represents love;[5] it could hardly be claimed, however, that all the flowers make reference to the kind of love Dante had in mind in the *Purgatorio*. When the deranged Dimmesdale encounters one of his many virgin admirers on the way back to town after meeting Hester in the forest, he fights an urge to "drop into her tender bosom a germ of evil that would be sure to blossom darkly soon, and bear black fruit betimes" (pp. 219–20). What all the flowers refer to in common is not love but passion, especially sexual passion: the red rose of her passion for Dimmesdale lands Hester in the black flower of the prison and later subjects them both to the black flower of Chillingworth's jealous mania. Passion may or may not have its own "consecration," to use Hester's loaded word, but such are the exigencies of social organization that excesses of passion will be restrained—even religious passion, as was learned by an earlier occupant of the prison and mythical procreator of the rosebush, the "sainted" Ann Hutchinson. As with the meteor, the flowers, taken as a group, are not only ambiguous or ambivalent symbols but they are in some respects devious and deceptive, like the world they are designed to illuminate or embellish. The flowers beside the prison purportedly "symbolize some sweet moral blossom" (p. 48), but they stand before and perhaps in a sense conceal the "black flower of civilized society."

To the extent that the characters function as symbols, they might be said to display a similar symbolic deceptiveness. Pearl and Chillingworth in particular are often seen, in Baym's words, as "symbolic characters": "figures of the imagination made real." What is meant is not that they are quasi-allegorical representations of abstract forces but rather that they function less in their own right than as part of the overall situation affecting the two main characters; thus Baym calls Pearl and Chillingworth "alter egos" for, respectively, Hester and Dimmesdale.[6] Pearl is more "symbolic" in this sense than Chillingworth, who does not fully assume demonic attributes until near the end, whereas Pearl's supernatural qualities do not diminish until the end: as Gary Lane observes, Chillingworth is progressively "unhumanized" whereas Pearl is climactically "humanized" by Dimmesdale's confession.[7] By then, of course, the story is over, so that most of Pearl's existence as a human is almost literally a postscript. During almost all the course of the book, then, she is a walking symbol. Moreover, she is a deceptive symbol, like the meteor and like the flowers, with which, as has been said, she is closely associated.

Like the meteor, she is explicitly identified with the scarlet letter, both by the narrator and by other characters (p. 102), and she partakes of the letter's impenetrable mystery and ultimate denial of all reference. Fittingly, when Hester asks "what this letter means," it is Pearl who provides the only satisfactory answer in the book: "It is the great letter A. Thou hast taught it me in the horn-book" (p. 178). In addition to an association with the letter, she also shares the deceitfulness of the meteor in its relation to concealed truth. As with the meteoric light, she illuminates the truth unthinkingly, acting out of an instinctive aversion to hypocrisy, "a bitter scorn of many things, which, when examined, might be found to have the taint of falsehood in them" (p. 180). (This radar for falsehood joins her with Phoebe, Hilda, and other Hawthornian innocents, with the important difference that her sensitivity finds a far more caustic expression in her "bitter scorn.") Thus she unerringly connects Hester's emblem with Dimmesdale's nervous habit of clutching at his heart (pp. 178–79). But also as with the deceptive meteoric light, the illumination that she provides reveals nothing to anyone who does not, or should not, already know—and even Hester at first misses completely the metaphoric validity in "the absurd incongruity of the child's observation" connecting the letter to Dimmesdale's heartache (p. 179). Indeed, her uncanny remarks might be said to conceal more than they reveal (again like the meteor): thus her repeated advances to Dimmesdale, who admits she causes him "alarm" (p. 206), may serve only to drive him deeper into his fearful secrecy. It is significant that the first time we see Pearl, as Hester carries her out the prison door, she is held in such a way as to "conceal" the scarlet letter (p. 52). Admittedly, to the degree the scarlet letter may represent the hypocritical social order that imposed it, having the baby cover it might be taken as a justifiable response, even as a protest. In a similar manner the seven-year-old Pearl takes an instant dislike to the jailer Mr. Brackett (p. 228)—his architectural name identifies him firmly with the structure he superintends—who had threatened to whip her mother when Pearl was a newborn (p. 71). Her detestation for one aspect of Hester's punishment (the jail) and her eager fixation on another (the scarlet letter) reflect not only the letter's symbolic multiplicity but also Pearl's symbolic duplicity: she seems to compensate her mother for her suffering but actually she intensifies it.

Pearl's meaning as a symbol is given one other explicit interpretation in the narrative: as the infant sucks at its mother's breast in the prison cell after the ordeal on the scaffold, its body is said to have "writhed in convulsions of pain, and was a forcible type, in its little frame, of the moral agony which Hester Prynne had borne throughout the day" (p. 70). The word "borne" cleverly underscores Pearl's significance as both a literal and figurative product of Hester's passion and of the "moral agony" that her passion leads to, not only for Hester but for the two men in her life. Pearl's symbolic relationship to both Dimmesdale and Chillingworth explains the curious ambiguity Hawthorne takes pains to cast on Pearl's parentage (although without, of course, ever really calling it into question). So when Hester and Dimmesdale get started on a homey little chat about which parts of their daughter's features come from which side of the family, he not only fails to pick up her hint about "whose brow she has," but after expressing his initial fear that all the world would know just from looking who had fathered her, he exclaims with relief that "she is mostly thine" (p. 206). Hester characteristically excuses his physiognomic myopia as an effect of his cowardliness, but as a matter of fact there is no reason to assume that Dimmesdale's assessment is inaccurate. Actually, it is more plausible to ascribe the resemblances Hester sees to a mother's fancy, because if Pearl really did have her father's brow, which is described as "white, lofty, and impending" (p. 66), his fears of being detected through his child's features might have had a rational basis after all.

We may then agree with her father that, at least physically, she is "mostly" Hester's. That instead of being black her hair is Phoebe- or Hilda-brown must be because, regardless of her preternatural attributes or occult powers, on the literal level she is still an innocent child: "in after years," when she has grown, her hair will turn Hester- or Zenobia- or Miriam-black (p. 101). Spiritually, though, she seems to have inherited some traits not from Dimmesdale but from her other "father," the one who could consider himself as the legal father and evidently does so, inasmuch as we learn at the very end that he has declared as his heiress "little Pearl, the daughter of Hester Prynne," also known as "the elf-child,— the demon-offspring" (p. 261). Until this lucrative transformation occurs she had been widely looked upon in the Puritan community as "of demon origin" (p. 100), and in a way she is of demon origin, since one of her spiritual progenitors is the quasi demon Chillingworth. Looking into her infant's eyes, Hester is understandably startled to see, not a souvenir of Dimmesdale, not even "her own miniature portrait" in reflection, but rather "a face, fiend-like, full of smiling malice, yet bearing the semblance of features that she had known full well, though seldom with a smile, and never with malice, in them" (p. 97). It is, of course, a prophetic image of the demonized Chillingworth. Pearl carries the signs of his mystical paternity because she symbolizes Chillingworth's passion for retribution and his moral agony to come, just as much as she symbolizes the sexual passion and moral agony of her biological parents. She is both a flower from the rosebush and the black flower of the prison it grows beside. As a symbol, she is associated with flowers because she shares with them the two-faced nature of passion, emerging equally as love and as hate, two equally passionate forces which, as we are informed in the closing pages, may even be "the same thing at bottom" (p. 260).

That phrase occurs in the context of reflecting upon the love-hate relationship between Dimmesdale and his tormentor, Chillingworth, who in comparison to Pearl appears more as a human being than as a symbol in a larger portion of the book and perhaps for that reason receives a surprisingly large share—surprising considering that he is the villain—of the author's sympathy. So even though he probably goes to hell, the narrator says "we would fain be merciful" and allow the hope that he and Dimmesdale, "mutual victims as they have been," may have found their "antipathy transmuted into golden love" in the "spiritual world" (pp. 260, 261). The posthumous reconciliation is presented as a sort of philosophical oddity (equivalency of love and hate), but modern critics have been quick to call attention to the homosexual overtones in the two men's attachment to each other. Crews characterizes their relationship as a sadomasochistic "mock marriage"; Allan Lefcowitz sees it as a "reverse seduction," with Chillingworth "counter-cuckolding" Hester.[8] Yet their interest in each other is to a large degree independent of their connection with Hester. After all, Chillingworth becomes interested in Dimmesdale before we are given any reason to suppose he suspects him: he simply likes him and would like to find out why he likes him (given his predisposition toward investigation) by learning more about him. The reason he likes him turns out to be the same reason he was attracted to Hester: like Hester, Dimmesdale has what the frosty Chillingworth lacks, "a strong animal nature" (p. 130). It works the other way round too: Chillingworth, like Hester, has what Dimmesdale lacks—a bold mind that gives the minister a "tremulous enjoyment," bringing a "freer atmosphere into the close and stifled study, where his life was wasting away" (p. 123). Along with her equally strong animal nature, Hester presumably had also been attractive to Dimmesdale on account of her greater "freedom of speculation" (p. 164), which, we might further suppose, could in turn help explain her otherwise unaccounted-for motives in agreeing to marry the freethinking Chillingworth, a man for whom she "felt no love, nor feigned any" (p. 74). In any event, the homosexual overtones can be exaggerated with regard to the relationship between Chillingworth and Dimmesdale. Were it not for the peculiar circumstances, there would be nothing intrinsically perverse in their friendship, just as there is nothing intrinsically wrong in the relationship between Dimmesdale and Hester except for the circumstance that Hester is married to Chillingworth. In this sense the possible reconciliation beyond the grave between the two men should be understood together with Hester's hope that she and Dimmesdale may spend their "immortal life together" (p. 256). It would be a heavenly ménage à trois, or rather a ménage à quatre, with Pearl, in one way or another the child of all three, reconciled to one father by his confession, to the other by his bequest, and to her mother by her penance.

Chillingworth has had his apologists, including famous ones (D. H. Lawrence, John Updike), despite the obvious fact of his becoming almost literally a monster. Nonetheless, Hawthorne wouldn't have kept the back door of heaven open for him if there weren't something good about him, something beyond a mere lex talionis claim to justice against Dimmesdale, which is not what I think Hawthorne has in mind—or at least not all he has in mind—when he calls the two of them "mutual victims." In addition to wronging each other, and perhaps opposing God, Dimmesdale and Chillingworth have each wronged themselves. Chillingworth in particular is a grievous, even pathetic victim of self-deception.

The most pathetic of his self-deceptions is explained to us in his own words. "Misshapen from my birth-hour," he exclaims in Hester's cell, "how could I delude myself with the idea that intellectual gifts might veil physical deformity in a young girl's fantasy!" (p. 74). The first time we see the husband and wife together, we get a painful insight into their previous married life as Hester, on the scaffold, picks out from the crowd a man who has one shoulder "higher than the other," despite the poor fellow's shift to disguise it "by a seemingly careless arrangement of his heterogeneous garb" (p. 60). It is the first thing she sees; it is the only thing she ever sees in him in a sense. Yet for that matter she may be the only one who really notices it: no one else ever seems to, except the narrator. She sees the worst in him, and not just physically. She suspects his motives even when he intends no harm, and perhaps to some extent she might therefore be accused of inciting him to contemplate evil (although at the crucial moment she appeals to his better nature to relent). She thinks he intends to poison baby Pearl and then to poison her, and when he does neither but instead heals them both, she feels that beneath his apparent kindness he may be acting out of "refined cruelty" in drawing out his revenge. "Thy acts are like mercy," she comments when he promises not to kill her lover, "but thy words interpret thee as a terror" (p. 76). Hester's phrasing is of added interest to us because she reverses the usual formula for a hypocrite, who customarily is someone of merciful words and terrible deeds. But then Chillingworth is not the customary hypocrite.

On an initial view he seems to fit the pattern of a pure or   55 medieval hypocrite—that is to say, a conscious dissembler who deliberately plays a role in order to attain evil ends, like Tartuffe or Iago. Like the former, he pretends to be "exemplary, as regarded at least the outward forms of a religious life" (p. 120), in order to enhance his power; like the latter, he continues to pose as a friend to Dimmesdale when in reality he has become the man's "worst enemy" (p. 171). But Iago and Tartuffe always know the truth about their inner selves—who they really are beneath the roles they assume—unlike self-deceiving hypocrites, who come to believe their outward appearances are real. Similarly, Chillingworth knows his adopted role for what it is, because he deliberately takes it up as a role: "he chose to withdraw his name from the roll of mankind . . . to vanish out of life" and assume a new name on the roll of mankind and a new appearance in life, which enables him to pursue "a new purpose; dark, it is true, if not guilty, but of force enough to engage the full strength of his faculties" (pp. 118–19). Yet the pointed absence of moral condemnation in this sentence is in keeping with Chillingworth's own morally neutral conception of what he is up to: "He had begun an investigation, as he imagined, with the severe and equal integrity of a judge, desirous only of truth." In other words, within his assumed role of "exemplary" Puritan citizen, Chillingworth sees himself as still true to his original identity of dispassionate investigator—whether scientist or "judge"—seeking only to ascertain the objective reality, "even as if the question involved no more than . . . a geometrical problem, instead of human passions, and wrongs inflicted on himself" (p. 129). The profound self-deception he gradually falls into originates in his failure to realize that he is no longer the "man of thought" he considers to be his core identity, a martyr to science who had sacrificed his "best years to feed the hungry dream of knowledge" (p. 74). He can't understand how, after plunging fearlessly into dangerous areas of knowledge such as alchemy and toxicology without harm, the study of "human passions" would prove any different. But it does, although he deceives himself into thinking he remains intellectually superior to passion. In a way this is another manifestation of the same self-deception that once led him to suppose he could overcome with "intellectual gifts" his wife's revulsion at his twisted body.

He deceives himself not only into thinking he still seeks only the truth but that in the name of truth his treatment of Dimmesdale is justified, even benign. "What evil have I done the man?" he demands of Hester, referring to the expert care he has been providing the minister (p. 171), and we have authorial assurance that with regard to "medical supervision" Chillingworth has been "doing his best for him, in all good faith" (p. 137). But as Hester told him before, his acts may be kind but his words are a terror, and now, without intending to, he proves her right, after she protests that Dimmesdale would be better off dead, by flying into a tirade that ends with a terrible moment of self-recognition. No longer able to deceive himself with his supposed devotion to truth, he suddenly stands self-revealed, in his own words and in his own sight, as a fiend. "The unfortunate physician, while uttering these words, lifted his hands with a look of horror, as if he had beheld some frightful shape, which he could not recognize, usurping the place of his own image in a glass. It was one of those moments—which sometimes occur only at the interval of years—when a man's moral aspect is faithfully revealed to his mind's eye. Not improbably, he had never before viewed himself as he did now" (p. 172). Unlike his brother hypocrite Judge Pyncheon—with whom he shares, among other traits, a knack for smiling and scowling simultaneously—Chillingworth is granted an opportunity to see through his self-deception. Denied such an opportunity, the Judge goes straight to hell, while the more fortunate Chillingworth, although ticketed for the same destination, is allowed, as we have seen, some hope for redemption.

The issue is left unsettled, but the terms are most clearly set out in this scene. "Dost thou remember me?" he asks Hester, with a genuine pathos in marked contrast to the travestied pleadings of the self-deceived Judge with Hepzibah. "No life had been more peaceful and innocent than mine; few lives so rich with benefits conferred. Dost thou remember me?" (p. 172). Again in distinction to an equivalent statement that might have been made about Judge Pyncheon, but only in sarcasm, we know that Chillingworth's insistence on his earlier goodness is truthful: even Hester would acknowledge that in the past his features, "though seldom with a smile," were "never with malice, in them" (p. 97). The Judge falsely believes he *is* innocent; Chillingworth truthfully knows that he once *was* innocent. So regretful are his memories of his lost innocence that they touch upon repentance, now that he is undeceived and can see how he has been a hypocrite not only to others but also to himself. Perhaps the possibility of his eventual salvation—no matter whether salvation is theologically or psychologically understood—is predicated on our acknowledging that maybe such a moment, or even a remorseful recollection of this moment, comes to him again before he dies.

But for now he immediately falls into another self-deception: that a "dark necessity" compels him to evil, thereby absolving him of responsibility. In this he resembles Ethan Brand, who deceives himself that he is beyond redemption. Both deceptions are deadly in that they easily lead either to defiance of God or utter loss of self, or both. Brand is lost, and in Hester's eyes so is Chillingworth, at whose retreating figure she proclaims aloud her hatred, not caring whether it is "sin or no" to do so (p. 176). However, we must take into account her tendency always to see him as worse than he really is, as now she indulges in the "injustice" of holding against him even their former "calm content," back when he was peacefully and innocently conferring benefits on mankind. In other words, we should regard her impassioned consignment of her husband to the devil not as an objective assessment of his condition but rather as "a dark light on Hester's state of mind, revealing much that she might not otherwise have acknowledged to herself" (p. 177). She, too, is not without sin; nor is she free from hypocrisy and self-deception.

Chillingworth's situation is notably more complex than that of most of the self-deceivers in the short fiction or to that of the later Judge Pyncheon. At the same time, the manner in which he and Pearl function symbolically in the narrative, considered alongside the deceptive nature of major symbols such as the meteor and the flowers, points toward Hawthorne's growing concern with the dichotomies of illusion and reality, and of life and art. In *The Scarlet Letter*, however, his main concern, I feel, remains the moral dimension of hypocrisy and self-deception, and his greatest contribution to our understanding of this dimension is embodied in the characterizations of Hester and especially of Dimmesdale. The ontological question raised by the study of hypocrisy—what is the real self?—also figures prominently, but it is always subordinated to a moral evaluation. With Dimmesdale in particular, the ontological question itself becomes a moral issue, as the real Dimmesdale can finally be characterized neither as a hypocrite nor as a saint, unless he can somehow be seen as both. With Hester the issues are not quite so extreme. Her fall into hypocrisy, though not excusable, is

58

understandable psychologically in terms of constraints placed upon the development of her personality, while her eventual triumph over bad faith is Hawthorne's most hopeful statement on the possibility of a mature, experienced human integrity.

The source for Hester that Sacvan Bercovitch believes he has discovered in Cotton Mather's *Ornaments for the Daughters of Sion* warns that a woman with Hester's endowments may, unless her behavior is "consistent with Vertue," "*Deceive* her self into proud Imaginations, and into an Humour, *Conceited* of her self, or *Contemptuous* of others."[9] Whether or not Hawthorne picked up self-deceptiveness as a character trait for Hester from this particular source, modern critics have, explicitly or implicitly, observed the tendency in her, most noticeably in the sophistic arguments she uses on Dimmesdale to persuade him it is morally right to run away.[10] The text itself similarly describes her reasons for not leaving on her own immediately after her disgrace—which is to say, the text qualifies the entire nature of her existence up until the forest scene—as "half a truth, and half a self-delusion," and the paragraph is constructed in such a way, no doubt deliberately, that it is difficult to tell which half is which. At the core of it—"although she hid the secret from herself, and grew pale whenever it struggled out of her heart, like a serpent from its hole"—is a yearning to be reunited with Dimmesdale, here adroitly alluded to as "one with whom she deemed herself connected in a union," "before the bar of final judgment, and make that their marriage-altar, for a joint futurity of endless retribution," like Dante's Paolo and Francesca perhaps. Whether we're meant at this point to approve or disapprove of the indication that her repressed love still has a sort of vitality, even if mostly in a negative sense, is hard to decide, inasmuch as "the tempter of souls" is said to be responsible for periodically reviving it in order to laugh "at the passionate and desperate joy with which she seized, and then strove to cast it from her." Closely connected is the half-truth, half-self-deception of her penitential ambitions, her confidence that "the torture of her daily shame would at length purge her soul, and work out another purity than that which she had lost; more saint-like, because the result of martyrdom" (p. 80). Instead of confronting her guilt honestly and coming to terms with it, she would transmute it into pride. What her denial or distortion of her feelings toward Dimmesdale has in common with her bad-faith project to become a saint and martyr is 59 that both self-deceptions entail lying to herself about what she really is.

The brief description of her later years in the final chapter (p. 263) may well suggest that Hester at the end of her life becomes what Baym calls a "mother to all, the Magna Mater"[11]—although in "The Custom-House" we also get as an alternative version that she "was looked upon by others as an intruder and a nuisance" (p. 32). In any case, her earlier life of abnegation is presented to us in the story as a hypocritical sham. The irony in this is almost exorbitantly rich. First, the hypocritical community singles her out as "the figure, the body, the reality of sin" and makes her into a "general symbol at which preacher and moralist might point, and in which they might vivify and embody their images of woman's frailty and sinful passion" (p. 79)—no doubt with considerable though carefully submerged titillation and sniggering. Then the public's hatred gradually begins turning into love, much "to the credit of human nature," because people are won over by her submissiveness, by her resignation to her suffering, and especially by "the blameless purity of her life," and they assume that "it could only be a genuine regard for virtue that had brought back the wanderer to its paths" (p. 160). But it is not a *genuine* regard for virtue at all: we have just been told that the effect of Hester's years as a pariah, far from improving her moral sense, has been to weaken her capacity "to measure her ideas of right and wrong by any standard external to herself" (p. 159). Yet the public systematically misinterprets the nature and intent of her "deportment." When anyone tries to establish personal contact with her, she touches the scarlet letter and walks on, a gesture that indeed "might be pride" but is mistaken for "humility." As a result, instead of the "common justice" Hester thinks is all she is asking for, she is given "more than justice." Most of the blame, however, rests with her that "society was inclined to show its former victim a more benign countenance than she cared to be favored with, or, perchance, than she deserved" (p. 162). She doesn't deserve it because the generous motives inferred by the public from her altruistic behavior are unrelated to her concealed actual motives, which are closer to vengefulness. The ultimate irony is that Hester, a victim of hypocrisy, is dangerously close to becoming as bad a hypocrite as any of her hypocritical persecutors, because her outward appearance of

charitable affection to all mankind conceals an inner reality of indifference. Her heart just isn't in it, and therefore her motives are impure. "Her breast, with its badge of shame, was but the softer pillow for the head that needed one" (p. 161)—but that is only her corporeal breast: on the figurative, emotional, or spiritual planes there was "nothing in Hester's bosom, to make it ever again the pillow of Affection" (p. 163).

The chapter in which these disturbing reflections are found is entitled "Another View of Hester," but the new view brings nothing new to bear on her inner life and in many respects reiterates the earlier "Hester at Her Needle," in which her career as a soi-disant sister of mercy is just beginning. As she stitches up fancywork for well-heeled Puritan saints and charity clothes for ungrateful paupers, she listens to "the insidious whispers of the bad angel, who would fain have persuaded the struggling woman, as yet only half his victim, that the outward guise of purity was but a lie, and that, if truth were everywhere to be shown, a scarlet letter would blaze forth on many a bosom besides Hester Prynne's" (p. 86). Her danger is not so much that she will come to believe the world actually is full of hypocrites but rather that as a result of such intelligence, like young Goodman Brown she will lose her love for humanity—and "Another View of Hester" shows how much nearer she is to doing just that. "Such loss of faith is ever one of the saddest results of sin," Hawthorne moralizes in the earlier chapter. "Be it accepted as a proof that all was not corrupt in this poor victim of her own fraility, and man's hard law, that Hester Prynne yet struggled to believe that no fellow-mortal was guilty like herself" (p. 87). As she drifts further into hypocrisy, the struggle becomes more desperate.

Not only must she struggle not to lose faith in her fellow mortals in the abstract, but as her hypocrisy deepens we sense in her a growing mistrust for the only individuals toward whom she might be expected to feel sympathy and understanding. Although her love for Dimmesdale is in hibernation, she has no reason to doubt his willingness to help her: after all, he championed her cause in the matter of keeping custody of Pearl, and he had even volunteered to share her punishment the very day it started, albeit he was speaking in a sort of code no one but her could decipher, and besides, he really didn't mean it. Still, she has no grounds for distrusting him. Yet part of the reason she decides to intercept the minister in the forest rather than visit him in his study is "that her conscious heart imputed suspicion where none could have been felt" (p. 182), which I take to mean that she is projecting her own distrustfulness onto him, just as she projects her own sinfulness— and her own hypocrisy—onto others. The word *conscious* further suggests a hardening of her lamentable condition, in that now her loss of faith is less a result of subconscious whisperings from the soul-tempter and more a question of deliberate, voluntary assent to cynicism.

More serious than her suspicion of Dimmesdale is her inability or refusal to allow herself to trust Pearl, who when all is said and done about the symbolic and supernatural trappings the character is burdened with, is nonetheless her daughter and moreover is an innocent child. Yet Hester spends the entire novel avoiding the obligation at least to try being honest with her. We have already noted how at their first appearance Hester presses the baby to her chest "not so much by an impulse of motherly affection, as that she might thereby conceal a certain token." She quickly changes her mind, not because she recognizes that her motives are questionable, but from "wisely judging that one token of her shame would but poorly serve to hide another" (p. 52), whereupon she haughtily brandishes the infant on her arm, as if instead of as a shield she would make use of it as a weapon. Similarly, "the turmoil, the anguish, and despair" the child imbibes a few hours later, with evident physiological consequences, while "drawing its sustenance from the maternal bosom" (p. 70), might not have been quite so toxic a mixture had there also been some motherly affection within that maternal bosom. On the symbolic level, the pattern of behavior thus so early established is related to the "morbid purpose" (p. 90) for which Hester designs Pearl's clothes: she identifies the child with the scarlet letter, and with more than symbolic justification, inasmuch as a child would have served as a sufficiently visible "token of her shame" for a woman in Hester's circumstances in a small New England town even today, perhaps—certainly as late as Hawthorne's time.

In psychological terms, however, Hester's poor mothering is another symptom of her hypocritical withdrawal from true human interaction while pretending, to herself and to others, that she is fulfilling her obligations to humanity as an altruist publicly and as a warmhearted single parent privately. "Thou art not my child!" she says to Pearl, "half playfully," but the child, who literally drank rejection in her mother's milk, sees through the "sportive impulse" and takes the statement "seriously." She asks that most profound and least answerable of childish questions—where do I come from?—and it is not Hester's stock answer but the "hesitation" with which she gives it that convinces Pearl something is being held back (p. 98). Here is a chance for Hester to show her daughter she trusts her, not by providing the name of the biological father—only her still rankling, because so long evaded, sense of guilt could have led her to suppose the child had any such thing in mind—but merely by answering the honestly asked question as every parent should: sincerely and from the heart. But Hester has already undergone too extensive a loss of faith to take such a chance. At a subsequent opportunity she does much worse: just as her suspiciousness of Dimmesdale has become "conscious," so instead of an unconscious "hesitation," this time we get her actual thoughts as she decides to dodge Pearl's inquiry about Dimmesdale's nervous habits: "No! If this be the price of the child's sympathy, I cannot pay it!" Of the dishonest answer she gives, the narrator comments that she has for the first time "been false to the symbol on her bosom," by which we also understand that she has been deliberately hypocritical to Pearl: indeed, her hypocrisy toward her echoes that of Dimmesdale, who tells Pearl during the nighttime vigil that they will all hold hands at the Judgment Day. Pearl laughs at Dimmesdale, no doubt because she finds his insincerity so transparent that there is no point in taking offense, but she presses her mother, provoking at last Hester's ugliest moment in the book. "Hold thy tongue, naughty child!" she snaps, "with an asperity that she had never permitted to herself before," and she ends (and the chapter ends) by threatening to shut Pearl "into the dark closet" (p. 181). Of course it is Hester more than Pearl who is in grave peril of losing herself in the darkness.

It is not that Hester doesn't love Pearl; it is that she is in danger of losing the capacity to love anyone and thereby of losing her love of life itself. Pearl is her best hope for a renewal of life and love within her: as she tells the governor, "Pearl keeps me here in life" (p. 113). But the narrator points out that in order for Pearl to accomplish "her errand to soothe away the sorrow that lay cold in her mother's heart, and converted it into a tomb," the child must be "entertained with faith and trust" (p. 180). As her hypocrisy removes her ever farther away from faith and trust, she is also removed ever farther from life   63 and hope. Hester's suicidal tendency, which perhaps finds a sort of fulfillment in the character's reincarnation as Zenobia, appears early in the story when she tells Chillingworth, who she thinks has come to poison her, that she "wished for death—would even have prayed for it, were it fit that such as I should pray for any thing" (p. 73). Especially for something inherently evil. "At times, a fearful doubt strove to possess her soul," we are informed much later, "whether it were not better to send Pearl at once to heaven, and go herself to such futurity as Eternal Justice should provide." Immediately after comes the famous one-sentence paragraph, "The scarlet letter had not done its office" (p. 166)—indicating that despite her outward saintliness, her inner desperation is so severe as to be life-threatening. Significantly, what induces her to put off the murder-suicide she is contemplating is not maternal instinct but her concern for Dimmesdale's well-being following the vigil episode.

Hester is saved—by which I mean she renews her love of life and her faith in humankind—when she ceases to be a hypocrite and reaffirms her true identity. The transformation is at first symbolic, then literal. When Dimmesdale refuses to forgive her for not warning him about Chillingworth, she impulsively presses "his head against her bosom; little caring though his cheek rested on the scarlet letter" (p. 194). This is the same bosom that for seven years has served as a soft but affectionless pillow for heads whose owners she didn't care about; it has been utilized, to be more explicit, as part of a revenge-inspired strategy to change the public perception of the emblem that is attached to it. Now her bosom is suddenly, almost miraculously restored—with "sudden and desperate tenderness"—to its function as a source and center of natural human passion, regardless of whatever labels a hypocritical society may choose to affix to it. As she holds Dimmesdale to her breast despite his vain efforts to break free, she can appreciate the difference between feeling a kindly regard for his prosperity and reputation— all she once thought she was concerned about—and loving him, even against his will, smothering him with her love, as it were. Yet the nurturing quality of her outburst of passion is attested to by Dimmesdale, who shortly after being so roughly womanhandled says to himself: "So powerful is she to sustain,—so tender to soothe!" (p. 201).

64   The symbolic restoration of feminine virtue to her breast is

paralleled by the equally instantaneous restoration of her physical sexuality. In a gorgeous paragraph (pp. 202–3) her hypocritical pseudo–nun's habit, given in synecdoche as "the formal cap that confined her hair," is removed to reveal the long-repressed woman within. In a virtuoso exhibition of female sexual imagery, the dark, abundant hair falls down her shoulders to create a chiaroscuro effect, "imparting the charm of softness to her features"; a playful, Mona Lisa smile "that seemed gushing from the very heart of womanhood" lights up her face; and a "crimson flush" is set to "glowing on her cheek, that had been long so pale." A race of hypocrites, afraid of their own sexuality and jealous of hers, had turned her into an asexual idol, and she, to her peril, had participated in her own dehumanization, but now, by another semi-miraculous "impulse" she has called back her true self from seeming oblivion. "Her sex, her youth, and the whole richness of her beauty, came back from what men call the irrevocable past," and the sky, the trees, and the little brook, availing themselves of the pathetic fallacy, exuberantly join in the celebration of her rebirth.

The next time we see Hester in her sister of mercy costume, as she waits for Dimmesdale to wrap up his affairs so they can decamp, she is no longer a self-deceiving hypocrite but rather a conscious dissembler, a trickster. In fact, she is actually impersonating her previous, phony self: her face is "like a mask" in that it is designed to mislead others, not herself any longer. Behind it the reborn sensual woman is thinking: "Look your last on the scarlet letter and its wearer!" At the same time, the narrator adds—rather apologetically, almost defensively—that she had some "feeling of regret" at leaving (pp. 226, 227), which I take not so much as a moral foreshadowing of her failure to escape but more as a suspense-building device, because Hawthorne knows that at this point we are on her side (if only temporarily) even though we recognize that her arguments to Dimmesdale that running off with her is the morally right thing to do are blatantly self-serving. We can infer from his uncharacteristically assertive (and embarrassed) "Hush, Hester!" that Dimmesdale, like the reader, sees through her self-deceiving assurance that their adultery "had a consecration of its own" (p. 195). She deceives herself in this regard so easily, almost (but not quite) innocently, because after seven years of isolated freethinking the Ten Commandments simply don't have quite the moral import with her that they still carry for him. That is why in the final analysis their failure to escape is a part of his story, not hers. Mentally, she has already left. Or to put it another way, they fail to escape because escape is an impossibility for him, not for her—except, of course, to the extent that escape *without him* is impossible for her, which was really why she hadn't gone away by herself in the first place, notwithstanding her self-deceiving rationale about working out her penance. The impossibility of her escaping without him also seems to be the main reason she comes back after his death. Had he died in Europe, she certainly would have stayed there. All the same, her having fallen in love with Dimmesdale was no accident: in other words, we shouldn't attribute her failure to find happiness and fulfillment in Europe with the man she loves entirely to her rotten luck in loving a man who lacked the audacity to throw off his old habits of thinking. His lack of courage, after all—his vulnerability—was precisely what attracted her to him, along with his repressed sensuality. The reason he disappoints her, then, is the very reason for which she chose him.

Her sexuality had been long repressed too, which was why she had once thought she could tolerate life with the misshapen Chillingworth, an illusion she might well have continued to entertain had not the affair with Dimmesdale showed her otherwise. Fear of sexuality entails a fear of life, and after again damming up her sexuality following her disgrace, her fear of life moved to the forefront of her mind in the form of a death wish. Once more an encounter with Dimmesdale revitalized her. But his death did not lead to further repression: there was no longer a need to repress her libido, since the only man who could satisfy it was gone. Yet the continued healthiness of her sexuality in her later years is evident from her effectiveness as counselor and consoler of women with amatory complaints (p. 263). She can help others to learn to enjoy their lives because she overcame forever her fear of her own life.

It is the normality of her final incarnation as a sort of colonial Dear Abby, more than anything else, that proves her ultimate success in freeing herself from hypocrisy. She again takes up the scarlet letter, and presumably she also reverts to keeping her hair confined, but she is no longer trying to prove to herself or to the world that she is anything other than what she is. The letter is an ornament—Pearl's great letter *A* in the hornbook—and the nun's cap is a convenience, while Pearl is her overseas daughter, not a token of her shame or an embodiment of her guilt. She tries to be helpful to people out of sympathy for them, not out of a hypocritical ambition to be taken for a saint and thereby avenge herself on all who once saw her as the "general symbol" of sin. Now some see her as the Magna Mater, others think of her as an old busybody, and she may be either or both. It is also known that she once became a mother, but she isn't a madonna or a whore, neither in her eyes nor in anyone else's. Waiting in the marketplace to board ship with Dimmesdale, she had looked forward to being able "to convert what had long been agony into a kind of triumph" (p. 227), and in her old age she does indeed enjoy a kind of triumph over hypocrisy—not only over the world's hypocrisy, but more significantly over her own as well.

FOUR

Arthur Dimmesdale:
The Hypocrite Saint

I MENTIONED in my introductory chapter that among modern investigators it is an unsettled question whether self-deception is intrinsically and invariably evil, whereas previously it was taken for granted that being dishonest with oneself was somehow always wrong. Yet it has always been open to question to what extent, if any, self-deception might be thought of as lessening an evildoer's degree of guilt, inasmuch as self-deceivers are also their own victims. For extremists, such as Matthew Arnold, one would expect there to be no mitigation; for moderates, like John Cotton, unconscious hypocrites might even be credited with having grace of a sort. It should be clear by now that Hawthorne was a moderate in this respect: the very ubiquity of self-deception in his fiction would suggest that he tended to regard it with some sympathy as a common human failing. He recognizes the evil yet pities the suffering it causes the guilty and the innocent alike. In Arthur Dimmesdale, who is Hawthorne's most profound study of a self-deceiver, the guilt he unquestionably acquires is mitigated and perhaps entirely overcome because the moral and ontological aspects of his self-deception so closely coincide. Indeed, Dimmesdale's confusion as to who he really is—which is his true face—virtually amounts to a psychological affliction, and the ambiguous death-revelation might be viewed, at least if it is taken positively, both as a redemption and as a therapeutic cure in which the patient dies.

In *Self-Deception*, one of the more respected contemporary studies, Herbert Fingarette puts forward a theory of self-deception that is also both moral and psychotherapeutic. With regard to morality, he characterizes self-deception with terms such as *spiritual failure* and *spiritual cowardice,* and he affirms that the "price" of deceiving oneself is "surrendering" one's "integrity." At the same time he acknowledges "the view that the self-deceiver is not to be blamed, that he cannot help himself, that he is sick, or deceived (in a way)." He reconciles the two views by proposing that moral judgments be held in abeyance until a person's self-deceptions have been removed by a process he calls "spelling-out," or "avowal of one's engagements," which means, briefly stated, making verbally explicit to ourselves our true and complete intentions at all times. "Such avowal," he claims, "is the necessary condition of moral action, but is not itself moral action."[1]

I bring in Fingarette not only because his half-moral, half-clinical account of self-deception will serve as a valuable reference when I turn directly to Dimmesdale but also because I feel that, just as Fingarette is offering us a theory of self-deception in general, so Hawthorne is presenting in Dimmesdale a self-deceiver who typifies all self-deceivers, which in effect means he is meant to typify everyone, given the pervasiveness of self-deception in the Hawthornian universe. As a personality, Dimmesdale is neither unique nor even extraordinary in and of himself. What is remarkable about him is the peculiar moral and psychological condition we find him in, but that is not his usual condition, which we intuit is rather normal or at least average more or less. Henry James probably is thinking of this banality in him when he says of all the characters in the novel that they "contribute little that helps it [that is, the story] to live and move," and they should not be regarded as characters at all but "as representatives . . . of a single state of mind," so that "the interest of the story lies, not in them, but in the situation, which is insistently kept before us."[2] That is why Dimmesdale, who is at the center of the "situation" and most nearly embodies all by himself the "single state of mind," need not be terribly interesting in himself—because his situation is so terribly interesting.

Not only is Dimmesdale interesting to us as readers because of his interesting situation, but within the world of the story he is interesting to other people for exactly the same reason, and for them as well as for us, it is his situation and not his personality that makes him interesting, even though most of the other people don't know it, whereas we of course do. Indeed he is interesting to them 69 precisely because they don't know his situation and can only see its effects on him, which they mistake for evidence of an extraordinary character. In "The Interior of a Heart" Dimmesdale is compared to his clerical colleagues and comes off second best in every category—scholarship, intellectual endowment, saintliness—except one, oratory: more specifically, his ability to move his hearers by his "sympathies so intimate with the sinful brotherhood of mankind." Yet this one professional distinction is a product not of his attributes but of his situation. "The people knew not the power that moved them thus" when they listened to a Dimmesdale sermon (p. 142). They don't, but we do. And we have no reason not to assume that if it weren't for his peculiar situation he would be a rather ordinary, if not a mediocre preacher.

His only character traits which seem separable from his situation, and which therefore most probably existed before the situation arose, are his repressed sensuality and his cowardliness—both ordinary characteristics, neither very admirable. Of these traits, cowardliness receives the greater emphasis. The first physical description of him sets off with attention-grabbing dashes "an apprehensive, a startled, a half-frightened look" (p. 66), and in his first speech he refers to Hester's lover as one "who, perchance, hath not the courage to grasp" the "bitter, but wholesome, cup" that she has to drink from (p. 67). (Incidentally, I suppose that this close proximity of Dimmesdale's "half-frightened look" and the adulterer's purported lack of courage is the first strong clue that they are one and the same person.) As detached from his situation, then, our picture of Dimmesdale's character leads to two conclusions. First, the nature of his character helps explain the mutual attraction between him and Hester, who was, so far as we are led to assume, the only person who was more than superficially interested in him earlier (that is to say, before his situation made him universally interesting). She, too, has a strong sensual nature that is also capable of being repressed, although her repression of it is probably rather more conscious and willful than his. A streak of personal pride may possibly be regarded as another similarity between them. The most powerful source of mutual attraction, though, must have been the complementary relation of his timidity to her boldness. When he calls upon her to reveal the name of her lover, she sees the fear in his face and hears it in his cryptic words, and the appeal from his cowardice to her courage is one she will always respect because it expresses the essence of their emotional union. (And even intellectually, it should be recalled, she is the bold speculator and he is the timid traditionalist.) Possibly at the end as he climbs the scaffold the elements of the equation reverse, even while he still needs physically to be "supported by her arm around him," with his courage for once prevailing over her cowardice. Possibly. Nevertheless, the nature of their relationship throughout the rest of the book is based on her acceptance of his fearfulness. At times this is shown with the consummate artistry of a writer who doesn't mind that it couldn't possibly register on the first reading, as when "Hester's situation" is described as "lonely" and "without a friend on earth who dared to show himself" (p. 81). Her one friend's lack of daring is something she has always understood. That is why he became her friend.

As I suggested before, the deeper significance of Dimmesdale's ordinariness and the absence of noble traits in his character (outside his special situation) is that he is meant to be a sort of Everyman: he is "representative," to bring back James's word, not only of a state of mind but also of the state of being human generally. To put it bluntly, if a fellow like Dimmesdale, a man like many others— above average but not much, hardly what one would call great although he is sensitive and fundamentally decent, yet given over on occasion to uncontrollable passion involving a woman—if such a man can become a hypocrite and a self-deceiver, and if he can then suffer horribly as a consequence, then the same fate might engulf any of us. Any of us might find ourselves in Dimmesdale's situation.

Dimmesdale's misery is of perennial interest because we all share it, at least potentially, so endemic is hypocrisy and self-deception among us. Dimmesdale is our stand-in, and his case is made especially acute so we can measure our own situation against his. Probably the most important single factor in sharpening his case is the theological sensibility with which he and his contemporaries in the fiction are imbued; nevertheless, the essence of his situation is independent of the theology. Kenneth Dauber is wrong when he argues that the "notion that Dimmesdale is a hypocrite . . . itself proceeds from a world where God and the devil are already established as parameters."[3] Mutatis mutandis, one might become a Dimmesdale-like hypocrite in Hawthorne's day or even in ours: this can be demonstrated simply by recasting Dimmesdale's problems in atheological terms, as in Charles Feidelson's dichotomy between the "private freedom" Hester urges him to pursue and the concern for "public order" he cannot bring himself to relinquish.[4] To insist that he would still be a hypocrite regardless of theology is not to deny the importance of his religiosity but rather to place it in some perspective.

If his religiosity is tangential to his hypocrisy, on the other hand, it is much more intimately connected with his self-deception. Dimmesdale could serve as a cogent illustration of what Fingarette has in mind when he writes of the "concern for integrity of spirit" in which "the movement into self-deception is rooted." This is something like an internalized or psychological version of La Rochefoucauld's celebrated witticism that hypocrisy is the homage vice pays to virtue, with the difference that the hypocrite uses the show of virtue to mask his vice in the eyes of others, while the self-deceiver becomes vicious only after persuading himself that his motives are compatible with what he sees as virtue. At some level the self-deceiver desires the good and thus does not deserve the outright condemnation merited by hypocrites. He may even earn our sympathy. "We are moved to a certain compassion in which there is awareness of the self-deceiver's authentic inner dignity as the motive of his self-betrayal."[5] In precisely this way we come to feel sorry for Dimmesdale, and yet Hawthorne takes Fingarette's basic idea and gives it another, much more disturbing twist. Here is a description of the effect upon his own state of mind of Dimmesdale's exquisitely hypocritical sermons in which he calls himself an abominable sinner in such a manner as to reinforce his universal acclamation as a living saint:

> The minister well knew—subtle, but remorseful hypocrite that he was!—the light in which his vague confession would be viewed. He had striven to put a cheat upon himself by making the avowal of a guilty conscience, but had gained only one other sin, and a self-acknowledged shame, without the momentary relief of being self-deceived. He had spoken the very truth, and transformed it into the veriest falsehood. And yet, by the constitution of his nature, he loved the truth, and loathed the lie,

as few men ever did. Therefore, above all things else, he loathed
his miserable self! (p. 144)

According to Fingarette, we feel compassion toward a self-deceiver
because his self-deception proves he has too much integrity to be a
conscious hypocrite. Hawthorne's moral objection to this would be
to ask about someone with even greater integrity—a constitutional
integrity that "loved the truth, and loathed the lie, as few men ever
did"—who for that reason is denied the "momentary relief" of self-
deception and is therefore left with no alternative to conscious
hypocrisy. Should we be more compassionate toward him or less? If
we have less compassion, then our renewed sympathy at the end of
the story might ingeniously be accounted for as our own feelings of
relief at Dimmesdale's finally having succeeded in lying to himself.
Such is more or less the opinion of William B. Dillingham, for
whom Dimmesdale is "a brilliant study in self-deception." "The
terrible irony of the confession," Dillingham explains, "is that he
dies believing it to be a completely open and free admission, while
it is hardly more specific than his earlier attempts."[6] Edward H.
Davidson makes substantially the same point in theological terms.
"The subtlety of Hawthorne's presentation is that the minister is
his own deceiver," Davidson writes; "he is that truly damned man
who convinces himself at every stage of his spiritual pilgrimage that
he is really 'saved.' "[7]

Admitting the possibility that Dimmesdale dies a successful self-
deceiver is difficult for us because it leads to the sad conclusion that
the only escape from self-deception is to move toward conscious
hypocrisy, the opposite direction from the one Dimmesdale would
then be seen as having taken. Yet only his death may have prevented him from retracing his steps. Had he survived his last
confession and seen he was still widely regarded as a saint, he
might have come to the same conclusion as Dillingham. To put it
another way, Dimmesdale seems to have an above-average gift for
engaging in what Fingarette calls "spelling-out," or making one's
inner motives explicit to oneself. Dimmesdale's aptitude for spelling-out ruined the efficacy of his earlier confessions as self-deceptions, and perhaps only his death precluded his spelling-out the
true intentions underlying his last confession. Indeed, he might
have arrived at the heartbreaking realization that his knowledge of

73

his imminent demise was what encouraged him to confess, or rather what impelled him to offer once again a sham confession, confident that this time the "relief of being self-deceived" would be eternal, not momentary.

Critics who wish to establish that Dimmesdale's final confession is in some sense (theological, psychological, or whatever) sincere and authentic are capable of going to astounding lengths to make their cases. Darrel Abel, for instance, acknowledges that the Election Day sermon "threatens to be his culminating hypocrisy," and the pages immediately preceding it reinforce that expectation. One such passage, in which Hester and Pearl comment on the minister's otherworldly air in the procession, Abel argues, must be read forwards and backwards, in effect, in order to understand how the threat of a culminating hypocrisy is subsequently circumvented. "Read anticipatively, with the knowledge given of the minister's moral history, he seems at this point to be a reinvigorated hypocrite; read retrospectively, he is shown to be a man inspired, who has received his 'vocation.' "[8] This is not far from saying that he really is what he himself believes he only pretends he is: he is a saint who thinks he is a hypocrite. Terence Martin does something similar with the Election Day sermon itself, arguing that it is one thing when Dimmesdale writes it and another when he preaches it, and in its latter mode it converts him.[9] Baym can't restrain herself from commenting on Martin's thesis, "God works in mysterious ways."[10] Of course, implausibility in itself is not a telling objection to an attempt to interpret a fictional episode that on some levels at least is purported to be semimiraculous: a providential reversal. At bottom it may well be that our interest in the question of whether Dimmesdale dies a hypocrite is of more importance than actually settling the question, even assuming that is possible. Roy R. Male endorses the pious sentiments of those "highly respectable witnesses" of Dimmesdale's last moments who insist on the minister's unblemished sanctity (p. 259), even while he concedes that such figures would, according to the "usual sense" in Hawthorne, be stock Puritan hypocrites whose testimony might therefore be suspect.[11] Whether or not his position is correct, by his willingness in such an extreme situation to trust the sincerity of even habitual hypocrites, Male expresses an undeniable and often admirable human need to remain faithful to even the barest possibility of transcending the human condition, notwithstanding either the weight of evidence against it or the inevitably impure motives of those who would keep faith. Even if it could be demonstrated that the charitable judgment on Dimmesdale of Male and others does not reflect what really is supposed to have happened in the story, nonetheless the generosity with which the judgment is rendered would not even then necessarily violate the spirit of the book, whose author, as we recall, "would fain be merciful" even to Chillingworth.

Highly relevant to any attempt to assess his integrity is the fact that there is only one occasion on which we are explicitly informed by the narrator that Dimmesdale has deceived himself. This is when he tells himself that his satisfaction at knowing he can still preach the Election Day sermon before running off with Hester arises from his wish that the people "shall say of me . . . that I leave no public duty unperformed, nor ill performed." "Sad, indeed," laments the narrator, "that an introspection so profound and acute as their poor minister's should be so miserably deceived!" Significantly, Hawthorne condemns on moral grounds this one self-deception with far greater severity and less sympathy than he condemns his continual acts of deliberate hypocrisy, even though he acknowledges that these were "worse things." Yet in contrast to his pity for the suffering the hypocrisy causes him, his tone in describing the self-deception is sarcastic, almost biting: he gives the minister a gratuitous taste of the torture he most dreads by referring to him as "this exemplary man," and he feigns reluctance to inform the reader of the sorry details in a caustically playful manner that foreshadows his mischievous taunting of Judge Pyncheon's corpse. The treatment is harsher because, unlike his hypocrisy, this self-deception is not a direct product of his situation, although the situation intensifies it. But the self-deception comes from the weakness of his character: in fact, nothing about him is more "pitiably weak" than this. In my diagnosis, the "subtle disease" Dimmesdale suffers from, which has "long since begun to eat into the substance of his character," is self-deception of the deepest, most unconscious sort, compounded by deliberate hypocrisy, and the prognosis calls for an ever-increasing confusion of identity: "No man, for any considerable period, can wear one face to himself, and another to the multitude, without getting bewildered as to which may be the true" (pp. 215–16).

The chapter in which this often quoted sentence appears is   75

"The Minister in a Maze," and among many other things it can be taken as an almost clinical illustration of a mind on the borderline between self-deception and insanity. As Dimmesdale's identity unravels, his impulses seem to be "at once involuntary and intentional; in spite of himself, yet growing out of a profounder self than that which opposed the impulse" (p. 217). He asks himself, "Am I mad? or am I given over utterly to the fiend" (p. 220), as a confused sense of self leads to loss of integrity, both psychologically and morally. In view of our post-Freudian grasp of the logic of psychopathological symptoms, Dimmesdale's incipient insanity can be seen as his only means of escape from an untenable mental state. But more is involved: the self-deception from which his madness proceeds is a product of his lifelong, largely unconscious repression of a "profounder self" that now emerges to incite him into blaspheming in front of a deacon and promulgating atheism to a helpless old lady who has nothing but faith in God to sustain her. Austin Warren's criticism of the chapter as "highly unlikely" should be considered alongside his misleading assumption that Dimmesdale couldn't have acted in such a manner unless he had once been a "young rake" when obviously he wasn't.[12] One need not have been an actual libertine to have deeply repressed libidinal or aggressive drives. Moreover, there is no reason to assume clergymen would be any less susceptible to urges such as Dimmesdale experiences than anyone else; in fact, it may be more reasonable to speculate that they would be more so. In his diary (which of course Hawthorne couldn't have known), Michael Wigglesworth reports ordeals similar to Dimmesdale's maze experience: "But above all my vileness breakes forth again whilest I am hearing the word. An Atheistic irreverent frame seizeth upon me; and whilest God is bidding me see his glory I cannot see it; vile and unworthy conceptions concerning god come into my mind."[13] In Dimmesdale's case in particular the repressed part of his mental life has much to do with his sexuality, as the protopsychoanalyst Chillingworth quickly discovers. Its most obvious manifestation has been his impulsive affair with Hester, although hardly less clear is his understated relations with "the many blooming damsels, spiritually devoted to him" from his congregation (p. 125); when he meets one such pubescent parishioner with a spiritual crush on him while he is lost in his private "maze," the reader is informed, with an audacious display of double entendre, "that the minister felt potent to blight all the field of innocence with but one wicked look" (p. 220).[14] Michael Small sees Dimmesdale's repression of his libido as his main characteristic and the Election Day sermon as "yet another denial of his 'animal nature,' another manipulation."[15] I agree that much of his character is determined by factors of this ilk; however, to attribute all his self-deception to sexual repressiveness would be to trivialize the novel by reducing Dimmesdale to just another sexually "uptight puritan." When I said that Dimmesdale is an ordinary man, I meant not that he represents the lowest common denominator in human experience but rather that he stands for all of us in a skillfully devised paradigm of a certain aspect of the human situation in the modern world. For this to be true there must be more to his personality than some garden-variety neurosis.

His repressed sexuality, in any case, would seem to have little to do with the specific self-deception for which Hawthorne holds him morally accountable, which concerns his motives for rejoicing at the opportunity to deliver the Election Day sermon before absconding with Hester. Indeed, to elope with the village adulteress the day after preaching the year's biggest sermon would represent a victory over sexual repressiveness and not a surrender to it, as well as a cancellation of his greatest torment, since he would no longer have a good name to hollowly mock him. I suggested earlier that such a turn of events would have fulfilled Hester's life perfectly, to our satisfaction as well as hers, if only Dimmesdale had been made differently, in such a manner that he too would be satisfied and fulfilled. But we are not told that his self-deception consists in persuading himself that he might after all change in accordance with Hester's expectations of him. Instead, we are told he deceived himself in not wanting to have it said that he failed to carry out his "public duty"—even if it were to be revealed almost immediately, as it obviously would, to the same public that his dutiful service to them was sheer hypocrisy. Yet apparently he believes he would still have done a good job even then. In other words, perhaps his nefarious self-deception consists primarily in believing that he can properly perform his duty—more pointedly, that he can fill his sacramental office—and still be a hypocrite.

That conclusion would be compatible with analyses of Dimmesdale that are more narrowly theological rather than psychological. (Not that the two approaches are mutually exclusive: one could, for

example, explain Dimmesdale's anguish as a psychological consequence of his dread of damnation without necessarily implying that
in the universe posited by the book salvation and damnation exist
in any other than a subjective manner.) Ernest W. Baughman, who
declares Dimmesdale's final confession "complete and genuine"
despite its lack of at least verbal specificity, emphasizes the theological ramifications of hidden sinfulness for a man who is in the
position of regularly both "receiving and administering the Lord's
Supper during the seven-year hypocrisy."[16] This is a telling point:
Dimmesdale's first manic impulse on his return from the forest is to
bring up "certain blasphemous suggestions that rose into his mind,
respecting the communion-supper," to one of his deacons. "He
absolutely trembled and turned pale as ashes," we learn, "lest his
tongue should wag itself, in utterance of these horrible matters"
(p. 218), and it is plausible to suppose him being moved to reflect
on the propriety of his participating in the sacramental rite at all—a
reflection he had no doubt been moved to frequently in the past,
given his peculiar situation as both a priest and a conscious if
unwilling hypocrite.

But on the other hand what priest, and particularly what Puritan
minister (given their introspectiveness), would not be questioning
always his worthiness to assume such an awesome responsibility?
Baughman takes as given Dimmesdale's unworthiness in the absence of his "complete and genuine" final confession, and yet, as
we saw before, it is possibly death alone that spares him from
determining his final confession to be as unsatisfactory as the
earlier ones. What, indeed, makes a confession complete and
genuine? Thomas Shepard, the greatest Puritan theorist of hypocrisy and self-deception, considers the difficult problem of the
efficacy of confession in his popular *Sound Believer* (1645). In drawing the familiar distinction between "particular sins," meaning
specific violations of divine law, and general sinfulness as a constant
feature of the unregenerate human condition, Shepard explains
that by a conviction of the former we arrive at a full appreciation of
the latter. Salvation however, arrives as a blanket redemption from
our sinful condition, rather than as itemized pardons for individual
transgressions: to update Shepard's medical analogy, when a sinner
sees "spots and tokens of death" on his skin so that he knows "the
plague of the Lord is upon him," he needs an internist to cure the
disease, not a dermatologist to remove the spots. Sins, then, are

particular, but sinfulness is general, and so are confessions of sinfulness such as "those confessions of the Saints" cited by Shepard: "I never thought I had had such a vile heart; if all the world had told me, I could not have believed them; but that the Lord hath made me feel it, and see it at last."[17] Dimmesdale's confessions—all of them—are at least verbally of this generalized sort; moreover, his knowledge of the particular sin that gives rise to them is acute, to put it mildly. His confessions are acceptable to everyone but him: he alone rejects them. When he tells Hester he has experienced "penitence" but felt no "penance," in Shepard's terms he means that he has not been made to "feel" and "see" his general sinfulness despite his constant preoccupation with his particular sin. Dimmesdale continues to Hester: "Else"—that is, had he felt "penance"—"I should long ago have thrown off these garments of mock holiness, and have shown myself to mankind as they will see me at the judgment-seat" (p. 192). At the end he does in fact convulsively tear away "the ministerial band from before his breast" (p. 255). Let us suppose that by thus defrocking himself he has successfully shown himself to all mankind in his final judgment-seat form. But as a saint or as a self-deceiver? Even if he had to the best of his ability undertaken to make plain (verbally or otherwise) his adultery with Hester Prynne, there is no reason in theology or anywhere else to assume that conclusive evidence of such an undertaking on his part would in itself be sufficient to answer the question one way or the other.

Unresolvable doubt concerning the state of one's soul, of course, is a source of anguish to all Puritans: maybe the unfrocked minister on the scaffold has succeeded in ridding himself not only of the symbol of his hypocrisy but also of the religion (in whole or in part) that has made his inner life an incessant turmoil. Michael J. Colacurcio, the best informed among Hawthorne critics about Puritanism, suggests that Dimmesdale at the end has largely "de-theologized himself" as the only means to escape "his old Calvinist entrapment." Colacurcio's reading of the novel, which seeks to parallel Hester and Dimmesdale to Ann Hutchinson and John Cotton, is fascinating and workable, although many might find it restrictive. Like Baughman, he proclaims Dimmesdale's reprobation, and his own knowledge of it, as all but certain up until the last scene, "when, of course, a major reversal occurs," and Dimmesdale is able to die with some hope of redemption because "he has got his doctrine down to certain saving essentials."[18] To say he has modified his theology is not much different from saying, like Baughman, that he has given up his "rationalizations about his usefulness as a minister,"[19] inasmuch as the "usefulness" of hypocrites is an important aspect of Puritan thinking on hypocrisy. However, unlike these theologically oriented critics of *The Scarlet Letter*, Dimmesdale never accepts the supposition that, for a man in his situation and with his beliefs, knowledge of his own perdition is unavoidable. On the contrary, he emphatically, almost contemptuously, rejects such an assertion when it is put forward in nontechnical language by a nontheologian, Chillingworth, who moreover frames his argument in psychological as well as theological terms by further accusing Dimmesdale of self-deception.

Because neither man knows at this point that the other is a hypocrite, Chillingworth's accusations are oblique and Dimmesdale's responses are abstract, but the drift is unmistakable to the reader, as it would have been to the speakers in retrospect. Chillingworth wonders if the weeds he gathered in the cemetery might have grown from a secretly guilty heart. Dimmesdale calls this a Hawthornian "fantasy" and goes on patiently (the chapter is called "The Leech and His Patient") to provide the physician with a miniature lecture in basic Puritan theology:

> "There can be, if I forebode aright, no power, short of the Divine mercy, to disclose, whether by uttered words, or by type or emblem, the secrets that may be buried with a human heart. The heart, making itself guilty of such secrets, must perforce hold them, until the day when all hidden things shall be revealed. Nor have I so read or interpreted Holy Writ, as to understand that the disclosure of human thoughts and deeds, then to be made, is intended as a part of the retribution. That, surely, were a shallow view of it. No; these revelations, unless I greatly err, are meant merely to promote the intellectual satisfaction of all intelligent beings, who will stand waiting, on that day, to see the dark problem of this life made plain. A knowledge of men's hearts will be needful to the completest solution of that problem."
> (pp. 131–32)

Intuiting Chillingworth's "shallow view" that confession is retributive, Dimmesdale explains that knowledge of particular sins is important as an indication of one's spiritual condition, which, however, owing to the inadequacy of our "knowledge of men's hearts," can never be completely fathomed except in a (metaphysically) absolute sense: "at that last day." Outside such a transcendent revelation, full disclosure of one's condition is impossible: "The heart, making itself guilty of such secrets, must perforce hold them." Looking ahead, the possibility is left open that at the end Dimmesdale, borne up by the "power" of "the Divine mercy," is able "to disclose, whether by uttered words, or by type or emblem," the secrets buried in his heart. For now, though, his condition is the normal one: he is forced to hold in his guilty self-essence.

Dimmesdale's arguments are hardly novel. In his "Farewell Sermon" (1750), delivered in circumstances not entirely unlike Dimmesdale's (both, at least, felt themselves to be under a cloud), Jonathan Edwards observes that not only do "ministers have no infallible discerning the state of the souls of their people," but neither "are the people able certainly to know the state of their minister." Among the clergy as well as the laity there may be prominent figures who are "grand hypocrites," pariahs who are "God's jewels," and of course self-deceivers, who "think of themselves, as his precious saints" but are really, "in a peculiar manner, a smoke in God's nose." Like Dimmesdale, Edwards must postpone the "infallible discerning" of one category from the other until the "day of Judgment," when "the secrets of every heart shall be made manifest" and "the people shall know whether their minister has been sincere and faithful, and the minister shall know the state" of his parishioners.[20] Dimmesdale would add, instructing Chillingworth, that the purpose of that ultimate unmasking is not vindictive but didactive.

Chillingworth tacitly concedes the theological point but immediately comes back with a psychological truth that Dimmesdale's own experience reinforces: the destructive effect of repressed guilt on mental equilibrium. Dimmesdale's explanation of why people thus allow their peace of mind to deteriorate is quite complicated, as his first words indicate:

> "But, not to suggest more obvious reasons, it may be that they
> are kept silent by the very constitution of their nature. Or,—can
> we not suppose it?—guilty as they may be, retaining,
> nevertheless, a zeal for God's glory and man's welfare, they

shrink from displaying themselves black and filthy in the view of men; because, thenceforward, no good can be achieved by them; no evil of the past be redeemed by better service. So, to their own unutterable torment, they go about among their fellow-creatures, looking pure as new-fallen snow; while their hearts are all speckled and spotted with iniquity of which they cannot rid themselves." (p. 132)

Insofar as Dimmesdale is alluding to the Puritan concept of the usefulness of hypocrites to the corporate life of the church, his argument is little to the point with regard to his own inner state. (That would be the case even if something more technical is meant, such as Cotton's idea of the unregenerate sharing in "federal" grace.) However, Dimmesdale mainly has in mind his sacerdotal function: he is claiming that a priest who knows he is guilty may still have the obligation to continue as a priest, and in that case he would not necessarily be a hypocrite. Admittedly, this line of thinking is more Catholic than Calvinist. Thomas Aquinas writes that even though a "religious or clerical habit" is a symbol of perfection, a man who "through human frailty" fails to live up to it "is not bound to broadcast his sin by putting aside the habit"; nor would he be a hypocrite if he continued to wear it, unless he originally adopted it "in order to pass himself off as righteous."[21] The essential question is the motive or "end" involved: perfection is not attainable by human means for any man, clergy or laity, Catholic or Calvinist. Some people, "by the very constitution of their nature," may be forced to live with the "unutterable torment" of hidden guilt and still carry out ministerial, even sacramental functions.

Again, Chillingworth would apparently concede that in an objective sense they might not necessarily be evil hypocrites, a word he never mentions. Instead, he capitalizes on the indeterminacy of human motives to accuse all such people of being at least potential self-deceivers:

"These men deceive themselves," said Roger Chillingworth, with somewhat more emphasis than usual, and making a slight gesture with his forefinger. "They fear to take up the shame that rightfully belongs to them. Their love for man, their zeal for God's service,—these holy impulses may or may not coexist in their hearts with the evil inmates to which their guilt has unbarred the door, and which must needs propagate a hellish breed within them. But, if they seek to glorify God, let them not lift heavenward their unclean hands! If they would serve their fellow-men, let them do it by making manifest the power and reality of conscience, in constraining them to penitential self-abasement! Wouldst thou have me to believe, O wise and pious friend, that a false show can be better—can be more for God's glory, or man's welfare—than God's own truth? Trust me, such men deceive themselves!" (p. 133)

A crucial question is whether the self-deception Chillingworth attributes to Dimmesdale is the same as the self-deception with which Hawthorne charges him later. Superficially they are similar in that both treat of his motives when he would "seek to glorify God," with Chillingworth speaking generally and Hawthorne referring exclusively to the Election Day sermon.

On closer inspection, however, the two views are in fact antithetical. In effect, Chillingworth is arguing that anyone who knows he is guilty is not only unworthy of God but incapable of in any way serving God, and therefore all who even try to serve God either are saints or have deceived themselves into believing in their sinlessness. Such a rigid, close-minded attitude toward redemption is compatible either with antireligious atheism, such as Chillingworth may well have professed in the past, or with the narrowest sort of sectarian misanthropy, such as Chillingworth seems to have embraced when he tells Hester that his "old faith, long forgotten," is coming back to him. Indeed, in accusing Dimmesdale of self-deception, Chillingworth sounds much like Hawthorne's typical self-righteous Puritan hypocrites, who think no one will be saved except themselves. Not coincidentally, after Dimmesdale dismisses Chillingworth's invective with a curt remark, they see Pearl dancing on "the broad, flat, armorial tombstone of a departed worthy,—perhaps of Isaac Johnson himself" (p. 133). In Edward Johnson's *Wonder-Working Providence of Sions Saviour* (1654), Isaac Johnson is the first mentioned death in Boston from among those who came over on the *Arabella:* his epitaph eulogizes him as "one of the Magistrates of *New England*" and, naturally, as a "crowned" saint in heaven.[22] Hawthorne's allusion to this first fatality takes us back to the beginning of the story, when he writes of the urgent necessity in a new settlement, however utopian its design, "to allot a portion of the virgin soil as a cemetery, and another portion as the site of a prison," and he states that in Boston the prison was built near Cornhill at more or less the same time the cemetery was started "on Isaac Johnson's lot, and round about his grave" (p. 47). Here Johnson's grave is linked to Puritan hypocrisy through its proximity to the prison; later the association is strengthened by Pearl, whose penetration of hypocrisy is instinctual, dancing on the grave almost immediately after Chillingworth's hypocritical speech about whose hands are or are not clean enough to be lifted heavenward. The entire exchange between the two men, we remember, began with Chillingworth brooding over the weeds he had gathered from just such a grave. A more direct indication of the hypocrisy in Chillingworth's accusation that Dimmesdale is a self-deceiver comes from his own mouth: he (of all people) ends his little diatribe by saying, "Trust me."

Whereas Chillingworth suggests that Dimmesdale is a self-deceiver because he continues trying to serve God as a minister, Hawthorne accuse him of self-deception for just the opposite reason: for thinking he can turn his back on his clerical responsibilities. In the past, Dimmesdale has been a good clergyman not only in spite of his hidden guilt and his consciousness of his hypocrisy, but precisely *because of* those very factors—because of his excruciating situation. When he then preached of how his sins tormnented him, he aroused feelings of compassion in his congregation because they could sense that his torment was genuine, however they may have misapprehended its specific causes. But when he leaves Hester to return to his study, he deceives himself into thinking he could still give an effective sermon after having agreed to end his torments by running away with her. His earlier sermons, though hypocritical in an objective sense because people took him for a saint regardless of his insistence on his sinfulness, were nonetheless beneficial because his motives were selfless and his only reward was the "unatterable torment" of bearing the hollow mockery of a good name. The price his cowardice forced him to pay, in other words, far outweighed what he gained from not proclaiming his adultery—an enhanced reputation, which in all sincerity was the last thing he wanted. For Election Day he plans the same sort of sermon as before for the same sort of people, not recognizing that it won't be the same if his motives are different, and therein lies his self-deception. As a case of self-deception, it fits Raphael Demos's formula: Dimmesdale believes both p, that he will give his sermon in bad faith, and not-p, that he will not give his sermon in bad faith—because he fails to distinguish the qualitative difference between his hypocrisy now and his hypocrisy then. He lies to himself that he is no worse a hypocrite now than he was before. It is a patent self-deception. Moreover, it is an evil self-deception. Even in Thomistic terms he will be an immoral hypocrite: for the first time he will be utilizing his clerical garb as a theatrical costume "in order to pass himself off as righteous."

To make clear the alteration in the moral character of Dimmesdale's hypocrisy, Hawthorne briefly reprises the earlier debate with Chillingworth at the end of "The Minister in a Maze" just before Dimmesdale rewrites his sermon. This time each man knows the other is a hypocrite, and every word they speak is packed with deliberately deceptive double meanings, establishing an equality between them in deceitfulness. Furthermore, this time Chillingworth's aspersions on Dimmesdale's sanctity meet no authorial contradiction: no Pearl dances on a Puritan hypocrite's grave. Dimmesdale utters his most hypocritical line in the book when he pretends to express his gratitude for Chillingworth's careful attention to his condition: "I thank you, and can but requite your good deeds with my prayers." Chillingworth's complex but devastating reply, comparing a "good man's prayers" to "the current gold coin of the New Jerusalem" (p. 224), not only insinuates a materialistic basis for Dimmesdale's spiritual services but also, as Frederick Newberry cleverly elucidates the passage, implies the falsehood and worthlessness of Dimmesdale and the entire religious and political worldview he stands for.[23]

Thus Dimmesdale is in a deceitful frame of mind as he resumes work on the sermon, and the sermon he ultimately delivers is false at least with regard to its content: Newberry, once again, points out Hawthorne's irony in having Dimmesdale prophesy "a high and glorious destiny" (p. 249) for the Puritan commonwealth.[24] Hawthorne's readers well knew that Hester's treatment at the hands of the saints was mild compared to what would happen to the Quakers, for example, under the leadership of the very same magistrates whose election Dimmesdale's panegyric for New England was celebrating. However, the falseness of the sermon is separable from the spirit with which it is delivered, and in fact

Hawthorne's description of its delivery seems much more closely related to Dimmesdale's earlier sermons about his private sinfulness than to the subject on which (as we learn a few pages later) he supposedly is speaking. Before, in the earlier sermons, we are told his heart "sent its own throb of pain through a thousand other hearts, in gushes of sad, persuasive eloquence" (p. 142). Similarly, as he preaches on Election Day his voice has "for ever in it an essential character of plaintiveness . . . that touched a sensibility in every bosom." Indeed, were it not for the subsequent report on its content, we would assume he is preaching the same sermon he has always preached, and in the same way. And in a sense he is, if not in the words he speaks then in the sounds he makes: "if the auditor listened intently, and for the purpose," he would hear, not a blessing on New England, but a "cry of pain," the "complaint of a human heart, sorrow-laden, perchance guilty, telling its secret, whether of guilt or sorrow, to the great heart of mankind; beseeching its sympathy or forgiveness" (p. 243).

That he can preach in the same spirit as before and to the same effect shows that he has not remained in the sinfully hypocritical state in which Chillingworth left him. He has stopped deceiving himself into thinking he could preach about his suffering at the same time he was planning to reject his suffering. But he has not, or at least not yet, escaped his hypocrisy entirely: on the contrary, he has resumed his earlier hypocrisy to the extent that he is once again allowing people to think him a saint while he assures them he is just another frail, suffering, guilty creature like the rest of them. Indeed, the universal perception of his sanctity is greater than ever. In a masterful display of verbal control, Hawthorne employs inflated diction to describe the universal perception without ever permitting the language to veer decisively toward pomposity (and therefore implicit sarcasm) on the one hand or lofty (and therefore confirmatory) exaltation on the other: "How fared it with him then? Were there not the brilliant particles of a halo in the air about his head? So etherealized by spirit as he was, and so apotheosized by worshipping admirers, did his footsteps in the procession really tread upon the dust of the earth?" (p. 251). We might comment: he is just as before, a hypocrite taking in the gullible, who are also hypocrites. But we might also say: he is just as before, a man for whom circumstances have provided both a rare insight into the limits of human tolerance for truth as well as a sympathetic appreciation for the suffering those limits inevitably entail.

It all comes down to his motives. Even if we knew for certain one way or the other whether he proclaims, verbally or otherwise, his adultery with Hester, there would still remain the question of his motives. In view of the imminence of his death, even making such a specific proclamation might be equally enhancing to his posthumous reputation as not making it. So it is right that we should be left in doubt: as Jeffrey L. Duncan nicely puts it, "Just as Hawthorne declines to describe the minister's breast, so he also declines to analyze his mind and heart."[25] Hawthorne doesn't know Dimmesdale's mind and heart, and neither does Dimmesdale, who, as we recall, is bewildered as to which is his true face, the one he wears to himself or the one he wears to the multitude. How can he know which face he wears at the end? How can anyone?

I can offer nothing more definite, or for that matter more favorable, regarding Dimmesdale's condition at his death other than to say that he surrenders to his situation. Loudly welcoming his coming "death of triumphant ignominy," he is tacitly accepting his departing life of public glory and private shame. Not that he has much choice in the matter: the "dark necessity" Chillingworth speaks of is real enough in the sense that no one can escape a chronic bewilderment concerning the truth of his inner nature. The famous advice we are given—"Be true! Be true! Be true! Show freely to the world, if not your worst, yet some trait whereby the worst may be inferred!" (p. 260)—is gratuitous as well as sententious, and that is precisely the point: we are not free to show our worst selves to the world, and yet, as Coverdale will be taught by Zenobia, the worst will inevitably be inferred about us on the basis of what we show even against our will. For the sake of truth, Dimmesdale dies while declaring his past hypocrisy and does so in such a way that he is taken by others as a sincere man, a strong candidate for redemption—a perception he explicitly endorses. Readers who disapprove of miracles and saintliness in their fiction are tempted to infer that he dies a hypocrite and a self-deceiver still. But even among this class of readers with an aversion to miracles, whether theological or psychological, there are very few who would deny Dimmesdale their sympathy. (Although there are some—most recently John Updike, who calls him "not the hero but the villain" and claims that "we rejoice in his fall.")[26] Most of us retain our compassion because Hawthorne retains his, even for a hypocrite and a self-deceiver such as Dimmesdale may yet be. No hint of irony colors the description of the crowd's immediate reaction to his death: the "murmur that rolled so heavily after the departed spirit" (p. 257)—nothing of the taunting follows Dimmesdale that will pursue the evil hypocrite, Judge Pyncheon. Unlike in the Judge's case, beneath Dimmesdale's hypocrisy and self-deception there is something that is not irredeemably evil.

To put the problem another way, the pressing moral message of Dimmesdale's experience may well be that a "death of triumphant ignominy" is beyond human attainment, and a frail mortal who sets himself up as a martyr to truth will instead become a paragon of hypocrisy. Only a metaphysical entity can be completely true: one might reasonably insist that Dimmesdale's claim is blasphemous as well as false by arguing that a death of triumphant ignominy is permitted to Christ alone. And yet all the same we might even propose to the contrary that Dimmesdale is truly Christlike because his sufferings are both representatively human and transcendently excruciating. We all share his misery, as I said earlier, but owing to the situation he finds himself in, his case is more acute, and so we can measure our own situation against his. Most of the time, fortunately, we simply ignore the hard fact that being true to ourselves and to others is all but an impossibility. But on those rare occasions when we are compelled to confront our own hypocrisy, perhaps we, like Hester, can draw from Dimmesdale's example the strength, or the grace, to overcome it, or at least, again like Hester, to renew our hope for humanity even in a world where bad faith is ineradicable.

FIVE

The House of the Seven Gables: Judge Pyncheon and His Brotherhood

WHATEVER APPEARS on Dimmesdale's chest might fitly be taken as an emblem of his true self, and after having completed an exhaustive exploration of the tangled depths of self-deception, Hawthorne has earned the right to present such an emblem in the form of an intractable mystery. In *The House of the Seven Gables* we are given a more explicit symbol of a central character's soul: it is a sort of hidden cesspool. Judge Pyncheon, compared to Dimmesdale or even to Chillingworth, is of course a melodrama hypocrite and a comic self-deceiver. His inability to recognize his own wickedness is meant to be ludicrous, and up to a point it is. But, the book as a whole is open to the same criticism as the cesspool symbol: it is meant to be funny, but it isn't quite funny enough. On the other hand, it demands to be taken seriously to some degree, and yet it is not quite serious enough either. Indeed, most readers would object to the romance not on the basis of its shortcomings as comedy but for its ultimate lack of seriousness.

"When we speak of 'seriousness' in fiction," Thomas Pynchon wrote recently, "ultimately we are talking about an attitude toward death," and he criticizes the characters in one of his early stories for "dealing with death in preadult ways. They evade, they sleep late, they seek euphemisms."[1] Much the same could be said of the characters in this romance, but the charge is weightier because, as happens often in Hawthorne, it is death that provides the definitive revelation of inner truth. Yet here Hawthorne's characters evade death even more childishly than Pynchon's: Clifford and Hepzibah, in fact, literally run away from it. The greatest evasion, however, is that of the book itself, which seems at least at times to be heading toward another deadly serious confrontation with death's revelatory power, despite the comic tone and melodramatic trappings. But we end up, unconvincingly, in a sunshiny world from which death and darkness have been banished forever. We feel uneasy because disturbing issues have been raised, and while we need not demand they all be resolved, we would not expect to have them simply ignored.

Among modern readers, at least, almost no one likes the happy ending. "Suddenly, we are back with an optimistic, progressive notion of things," runs a recent, typical complaint, by Richard Gray. "The Judge is dead and quickly forgotten; the house is abandoned; Clifford, Hepzibah and company all change for the better. Nearly everyone, including the narrator, seems to wash his hands of the past." A possible dark spot, Holgrave's volte-face from radical firebrand to timid conservative, "looks to be little more than a tattered flag held aloft while the author sounds the retreat."[2] Nina Baym tries to make something more profound of Holgrave's apostasy: transformed by "death itself," Holgrave becomes a "sad man" who "accepts" his fate "with weary melancholy." I can't go along with this quasi-tragic Holgrave for the simple reason that he gets the girl, and not just any girl, but angelic Phoebe, who, far from being the mere source of "solace and protection" Baym makes her out to be,[3] is one of Hawthorne's perfectly virtuous virgins—too perfect to be believable, as Hawthorne may have realized. When all-knowing Uncle Venner compares her to "one of God's angels," the narrator admits the "eulogium" might be "too high-strained," and yet he proceeds to elaborate upon it and then goes on, as if seeking a counterbalance, even more improbably to compare Hepzibah to an angel as well, albeit to the one Jacob wrestled with (2:82). Clearly Holgrave is not to be overly pitied for winning such a creature as Phoebe, regardless of his incidental misgivings about joining the Establishment.

Yet Baym is correct in calling attention to a vague sense of despondency clinging to Holgrave after the Judge's death, but I think she came closer to putting her finger on its cause in an earlier version of her analysis, in which she said that "at the moment he takes the name of Maule, Holgrave becomes in fact a Pyncheon."[4] Roy R. Male may have been noting something similar in his observation that in the process of spending an hour with Judge

Pyncheon's corpse Holgrave "discovers himself."[5] I would make the same remark, but I'd mean it a little differently. At the end of the novel, we learn that this son of the Maules has all along been pretending to be many things he really is not: a Holgrave, a free spirit, an artist, a reformer, and so on. He becomes a Pyncheon in the sense that he, like the dead Judge, has been exposed as a kind of hypocrite. Unlike the Judge, Holgrave is made aware of his deceptiveness. "You should have known sooner," he confesses to Phoebe in his last speech, adding parenthetically, and lamely, "(only that I was afraid of frightening you away)" (p. 316). His growing conviction that he has been wrong to dissemble before people he has grown to love is what accounts for his uneasiness in the latter part of the book. But at the same time, his capacity to recognize the truth about himself—that, despite his radical posturing, he is no different from anyone else with regard to his personal desires—bodes well for his future wedded bliss with the personification of feminine purity, whose "poise," as he had put it in his love declaration to her earlier, "will be more powerful than any oscillating tendency of mine" (p. 307).

Holgrave's oscillations between different opinions and identities represent an extreme case of a common condition. Phoebe's unconscious integrity makes her unique, the sole exception to a general rule in the world of this novel that people are not what they present themselves as and see themselves to be. There is always a discrepancy perceptible to the reader, not only in individual characters but in the aggregate population as well. In the Preface Hawthorne pleads romantic license for seeming to bring "discredit" on the "venerable town" of Salem (p. 3), and with good reason, since beneath the respectable exterior he shows us a rather brutal place. Most of our views of the populace are centered around the house and particularly Hepzibah's cent shop, which attracts an unpleasant class of customers. The "cannibal-feast" in gingerbread of her first paying customer (p. 50) is of course too precious to be taken symbolically, but there is nothing sentimentalized about the battered wife who comes in later: "one of those women, naturally delicate, whom you at once recognize as worn to death by a brute— probably a drunken brute—of a husband, and at least nine children." The drunken brute in question also comes in and joins a string of dissatisfied shoppers, including a "little girl" and a "very capable housewife," who return purchases, act surly, and deliver insults either out loud or by "spitefully" slamming doors and other objects (pp. 52–53).

Other residents of the neighborhood are hardly more civil. The story is framed between conversations of one "Dixey" with an unnamed companion, who at the beginning predict Hepzibah's imminent failure (p. 47), reiterate this analysis after the Judge's death, and also speculate on Hepzibah's complicity in the murder (pp. 291, 296), and in the final pages exhibit their jealousy at her ultimate good fortune (pp. 318–19). Yet these two no doubt think themselves upstanding, God-fearing citizens with nicer than average consciences and charitable dispositions. "It seems a sin to be the first" to say the Judge is dead, whispers the nameless of the two as circumstances begin pointing to that conclusion (p. 296), so careful is he not to think ill of anyone important, and yet he declares himself willing to accept Hepzibah's sudden enrichment only as a stroke of unmerited luck, for "if we are to take it as the will of Providence, why, I can't exactly fathom it" (p. 318). Very likely the pair of them were among the spies the Judge tells Hepzibah he has set to watching the house. An ample supply of them was easily recruited, including the "butcher, the baker, the fishmonger, some of the customers of your shop, and many a prying old woman" (p. 236). (Presumably the candlestick maker declined to join the informers because whale oil lamps have rendered him obsolete and not because he is sympathetic to the inhabitants of the house.) There is scant sympathy for Clifford and Hepzibah from one of the spies, the butcher, who publicly proclaims that it is "demeaning a man's business to trade with such people" (p. 292). Perhaps we are to imagine him saying this with his hands dripping blood and gore. In any event, we get the idea that the whole town is infested with hypocrites from the way the old brother and sister are held in low esteem while their unsavory cousin is respected and admired, whereas our feelings go just the other way. "And who but a blood-relation, that couldn't help himself," asks Mrs. Gubbins's prying old neighbor, in reference to the Judge's supposed generosity toward his poor relatives, "would take in that awful-tempered Old Maid, and that dreadful Clifford?" (p. 289). We know who is really dreadful and awful-tempered, and we also know why the townspeople are capable of being deceived by appearances. It is no innocent deception, not even on their part.

92   Naturally, we have an advantage over the townspeople in that we

are told both explicitly and implicitly that Hepzibah's gruff exterior hides a soft and kind interior, so that by the time we arrive at the chapter entitled "The Scowl and Smile," we know without being told that Hepzibah's scowl is no truer an indication of her inner nature than is the Judge's smile. We know even if no one else does, not even the two characters involved. We are informed with regard to Hepzibah's frown the first time it is mentioned that "she had been led to interpret the expression almost as unjustly as the world did," a self-deception of a forgivable sort arising from feelings of inferiority, just as the frown itself "was the innocent result" of inferior eyesight. But in fact, "her heart never frowned" (p. 34), and we see her performing humane acts, such as giving the abused wife extra flour without charging for any of it—acts that don't do a thing to alter her reputation for being an ogre because it is not with the end of improving her reputation in mind that she performs them. Obviously, this helps set us up for her cousin Jaffrey, whose charitable enterprises are all ploys, and whose heart never smiles.

Hepzibah's heart is basically sound, but that doesn't make her a wrinkled, (merely) physically ugly version of Phoebe. She is also a self-deceiver of long standing in the less excusable sense of cling-ing to her aristocratic pretensions. It is this attitude that we are to understand has ruined her life's happiness even more, perhaps, than have unfortunate circumstances or her cousin's villainy. In the shop-opening sequence she is forced to unmask, to "stand revealed in her proper individuality," and we learn that her fate consists not in a high tragedy of ruined magnificence, but rather in a mundane "great life-trial" of an ordinary person who, "after sixty years of idleness," "finds it convenient to earn comfortable bread by setting up a shop, in a small way" (pp. 40, 41). She is well rid of the debili-tating self-deception: "better to be a true woman, than a lady," Holgrave consoles her (p. 45), with the democratic implication that to say "false lady" would be a redundancy. She doesn't come around to a healthier view of these matters instantly, though, as we infer from the unrighteous indignation she enviously expresses at the sight of a "real" lady who does nothing more provocative than walk down the street smelling of money. But we know Hepzibah will ultimately be delivered of her one evil tendency because she immediately begs God's forgiveness, "ashamed and penitent." "Doubtless, God did forgive her," says Hawthorne (p. 55), and so does he, and so do we.

We need not dwell on Clifford because his situation is similar to his sister's, regarding both the nature of his self-deception and his prospects for redemption. He is also a case of arrested development, although he can't be blamed as much as Hepzibah since his lifelong isolation was involuntary. However, having had a good excuse for not growing up before is no excuse for not growing up now that he is back in circulation. But growing up means accepting yourself for what you really are, and Clifford has as much difficulty in this as Hepzibah. "He cannot endure his identity as a broken, aging man," explains Richard Harter Fogle, so he tries to lose himself in soap-bubble delusions.[6] The reader quickly learns to view his behavior more as childish selfishness than as childlike innocence, as it may have first appeared. Nevertheless, in the abortive church going episode we see that Clifford, like Hepzibah, is not a lost soul. "In the incident now to be sketched," announces the narrator in a curious instance of what might be called anticipatory self-interpretation, "there was a touching recognition, on Clifford's part, of God's care and love towards him—towards this poor, forsaken man, who, if any mortal could, might have been pardoned for regarding himself as thrown aside, forgotten, and left to be the sport of some fiend" (p. 167). Clifford receives the same authorial pardon for his childish delusions and selfish desires that Hepzibah receives for her aristocratic delusions and envious impulses.

Having been pardoned separately, they are granted absolution together when they pray to God for mercy at the climax of the train episode. They get it, too: when we next see them, Phoebe rejoices at their return by saying "Thank God!" twice, and they both echo the sentiment. In coming back to their home they demonstrate their ability to accept themselves at last for what they are and to accept the rest of the human race for what it is. Hepzibah has long been "peopling the world with ugly shapes," as Holgrave tells her (p. 44), while Clifford has absurdly magnified the magnificence of the passing parade by viewing it with his soap-bubble vision from the ennobling perspective of the "arched window" (p. 165). That they have learned to think of other people as differing from themselves only in the greater or lesser degree of their human frailty is one of the themes of Clifford's extraordinary lecture in the railroad car. Against the gimlet-eyed old curmudgeon who considers everything a humbug, Clifford argues for tolerance and understanding, even for bank robbers, "who, after all, are about as honest as nine people in ten, except that they disregard certain formalities." No one should be scorned merely for seeming other than what he is, because that condition is all but universal; paradoxically, admitting that it applies to oneself is the nearest approach to sincerity. When the curmudgeon, "bringing his gimlet-eye to a point on Clifford, as if determined to bore right into him," complains, "I can't see through you," Clifford laughingly admits the fact but adds: "And yet, my dear Sir, I am as transparent as the water of Maule's Well!" (p. 265). This echoes the narrator's description of him a few pages earlier, when he was in the midst of his monologue: "a youthful character shone out from within, converting the wrinkles and pallid duskiness of age into an almost transparent mask" (p. 260). Now more than ever Clifford is not what he seems to be, but this time, in a reversal similar to what we encountered in certain of the tales, what appears to be real—Clifford as old man—is shown to be a mask, while the supposed illusion of youth comes true in a deeper sense. "But now do I look old?" asks Clifford, and in responding to his own question he makes the paradox explicit: "If so, my aspect belies me strangely; for—a great weight being off my mind—I feel in the very hey-day of youth, with the world and my best days before me!" (p. 262). Through taking himself and the world as they really are, his life has been renewed, and the child role that before he had poorly acted is now a genuine expression of his spirit.

Notwithstanding the misgivings of Dixey's friend, the splendid rewards showered on Clifford and Hepzibah at the end are in keeping with the ways of providence not only because of their repentance but also because they were, after all, the only victims of their deceits. This brings us back to the problem of Holgrave's final status: his melancholy, his reluctant conversion to supporting the status quo, his identification with the spirit of the Pyncheons. Like his future in-laws, he too has arrived at self-realization, but unlike them he has not yet found the way to repentance and forgiveness. With angelic Phoebe beside him and the beatified Alice taking up the matter in heaven, we can be confident his redemption is only a question of time; in the meanwhile, however, he is going to have to live with guilt . . . specifically, his guilt over having spent the entire book deceiving everyone in it.

It might be argued that the end Holgrave reaches justifies the deceitful means by which he gets there, but it is more to Holgrave's credit that Hawthorne never has him even faintly hint at such a self-serving excuse, nor is it ever put forward in the narrative, not even by indirection. Moreover, in looking back over Holgrave's behavior we discover subtle but unmistakable indications of authorial disapproval. Encouraging Hepzibah to go ahead with her little enterprise of the cent shop, Holgrave says: "If the Pyncheons had always acted so nobly, I doubt whether the old wizard Maule's anathema, of which you told me once, would have had much weight with Providence against them." Disregarding the literally accurate but patently dishonest implied explanation of how he learned of the curse, such words in the mouth of a Maule virtually constitute a repetition and renewal of the craving for vengeance— and indeed the curse is again fulfilled. Hepzibah's unconsciously ironic reply, about how gratifying her predicament would be to "old Maule's ghost, or a descendant of his," probably does no more than amuse that very descendant standing before her, since he believes (correctly) that opening the shop will be a good thing for her. However, the unconscious irony of her next remark, as she refuses payment for the biscuits he takes, bitingly exposes the essential duplicity of Holgrave's position: "A Pyncheon must not, at all events, under her forefathers' roof, receive money for a morsel of bread, from her only friend!" (pp. 45–46).

Hepzibah has no inkling of Holgrave's true character, but Phoebe is aware of something fishy from the beginning. "She did not altogether like him," we are told. "She rebelled, as it were, against a certain magnetic element in the artist's nature, which he exercised towards her, possibly without being conscious of it" (p. 94). Phoebe wouldn't exactly be "conscious" of it either, but as part of her virginal purity she has an infallible built-in radar for evil and reacts to its presence as if by instinct—a trait most strikingly displayed when she shies away from Judge Pyncheon's proffered lips "without design, or only with such distinctive design as gives no account of itself to the intellect" (p. 118). The locus of evil in Holgrave is precisely that "magnetic element" Phoebe instinctively rebels against, for whether he does so deliberately or not, Holgrave puts himself in a position to exert the same psychosexual mastery over Phoebe that the demonic Westervelt uses to enslave Priscilla in *The Blithedale Romance*.[7] But Phoebe submits to him eventually, perhaps because at an even deeper level she is also instinctively aware that Holgrave is not a reprobate. And she is right: he doesn't spiritually rape her the way Matthew Maule violated Alice Pyncheon's undesigning interest in him. "Let us allow him integrity," comments the narrator on Holgrave's forbearance, "forever after to be confided in" (p. 212).

A yet stronger endorsement of his fundamental integrity occurs significantly in a preliminary explanation of why his outward aspect seems so uncertain if not volatile. (The complete explanation, that he is really not who he claims to be, is of course reserved until the end of the book.) We are informed that even though he has spent much of his life not just changing jobs but really shifting roles— "putting off one exterior, and snatching up another, to be soon shifted for a third"—nonetheless "he had never violated the innermost man, but had carried his conscience along with him" (p. 177). This, at any rate, is what we are meant to think of Holgrave, although I tend to agree with Marcus Cunliffe's criticism that, with respect to Hawthorne's skill in the art of constructing fictional characters, Holgrave emerges more as an "Identi-Kit of Hawthornian types" than as "a recognizable human being."[8] But Hawthorne can be partly forgiven by our conceding that he was working with quasi-mythic materials; as Henry James first observed, Holgrave "is an attempt to render a kind of national type."[9] He represents the characteristically American figure of the self-reliant man, who in Emerson's rendering of the myth is a "sturdy lad from New Hampshire or Vermont, who in turn tries all the professions, who *teams it, farms it, peddles*, keeps a school, preaches, edits a newspaper, goes to Congress, buys a township, and so forth, in successive years, and always like a cat falls on his feet."[10] A twentieth-century version of the same basic idea would be Erik Erikson's concept of "Protean man," of which the multifaceted Thomas Jefferson is the grand embodiment.[11] The self-reliant or Protean figure shares with Holgrave the "most remarkable . . . fact that, amid all these personal vicissitudes, he had never lost his identity" (p. 177). This never-lost identity is that of the Young American, a popular catchphrase Hawthorne may well have had in the back of his mind for Holgrave, who "might fitly enough stand forth as the representative of many compeers in his native land" (p. 181).

In seeking to add flesh and blood to the catchphrase or myth, Hawthorne's novelistic instinct led him to mix in an element of mystery and even a hint of evil. Thus alongside the allusions to "men with long beards," "community-men and come-outers," and other "banditti-like associates" vaguely connected with Holgrave, we also get a few judiciously calculated descriptions like this one: "Nevertheless, in the artist's deep, thoughtful, all-observant eyes, there was now-and-then an expression, not sinister, but questionable; as if he had some other interest in the scene than a stranger, a youthful and unconnected adventurer, might be supposed to have" (p. 156). If only Hawthorne had allowed him to be just a little more sinister, Holgrave might have turned out a memorable character; as it is, he is merely questionable. At times he is even wishy-washy: the reason he recites his Alice Pyncheon story to Phoebe is to avoid the challenge of "directly answering her" when she twice inquires "why he now chose to lodge in the desolate old Pyncheon house" (pp. 182, 184). Baym sees in Holgrave "a contrast, in his artistry, to previous Maules, in whom artistic energies were perverted"; however, surely it is perverse to use art as a means to evade the truth. His evading Phoebe's question is a repetition of his earlier duplicity with Hepzibah, and the consequences this time are much more dangerous as the story becomes the means of mesmerizing the girl. It is curious that on the same page on which Baym declares Holgrave to be "a kind of archetypal artist, for he has mastered a variety of media and is unattached to his productions," she also takes note of Hawthorne's "one doubt about this otherwise admirable character"—that he may end up as just another flash in the pan (p. 181)— but she makes no effort to connect the two observations.[12] Far from being master of a variety of media, I would describe Holgrave as a mere dabbler: a contributor to women's magazines and a run-of-the-mill portrait photographer who by his own admission mostly produces pictures that "look unamiable" (p. 91). At the end of the novel there isn't the slightest hint of his ever amounting to anything more than a well-heeled nonentity: he is last referred to as "the descendant of the legendary wizard," which is his one remaining distinction. As I said before, he feels guilt over his past dishonesty, although given his commendable habit of always carrying his conscience along with him, we assume his guilt will be surmounted in time. It is all so vague because Hawthorne didn't arrange for the guilt to be more substantial. The fact is, we never do get a straight answer to Phoebe's question about what exactly Holgrave is up to, though I'd like to think something of his motives can be inferred from one of his remarks to Phoebe at the time:

"The house ought to be purified with fire—purified till only its ashes remain" (p. 184)—an unchristian but not unfitting revenge for the witches to seek against their executioners. Had Holgrave been explicitly contemplating something along such incendiary lines, his deceitfulness would have been a weightier matter, and his subsequent guilt and need for absolution more substantial. He might even have gone on to become a serious artist, just as Roderick Elliston went on to write "allegories of the heart" after experiencing the bosom serpent. But the romance as a whole ultimately evades seriousness in the same manner Holgrave evades unpleasant truths, by telling a pretty story, and the photograph of the late Judge Pyncheon will no doubt be Holgrave's final contribution to art. At least it will serve as a reminder to him of the evils of hypocrisy.

The dead man's picture is also an appropriate cap to Holgrave's artistic career in that it proves his previous failures with the same subject when he was alive are not entirely attributable to his admitted ineptness at attaining portraits that will satisfy his customers. Earlier he had told Phoebe of taking the Judge "over and over again" in the hope of producing a "likeness" suitable for engraving. But notwithstanding the young daguerreotyper's pronouncements on the sun's "wonderful insight" into the "secret character" of a face and on the lack of "flattery" in his "humble line of art," the results have been so unlike the subject's manifest appearance as to require tedious multiple sittings (pp. 91, 92). So it is with a sense of professional vindication that he later presents Phoebe with another shot of "the same face." And when she recognizes that this is a death-portrait, he triumphantly proclaims, "Such as there represented, . . . he sits in the next room" (p. 302). Now he looks exactly like his picture, which proves that the reason he didn't before had nothing to do with distortions caused by Daguerre's newfangled technology. Or to put it another way, death has fixed the Judge's character just as a photograph fixes one's image, once and for all and without the often deceptive patina produced by movement and animation. His public image undergoes a similar posthumous revaluation (p. 310). The preternaturally sensitive may also catch a glimpse of the Judge's real features in the Maule-enchanted looking glass, where by "a sort of mesmeric process" the "departed Pyncheons" appear as their true sinful selves and "not as they had shown themselves to the world" (p. 21). 99

Like a hypocrite in Wigglesworth's graveyard in "Chippings with a Chisel," Judge Pyncheon's true character comes out only in death. He is quite literally the last to know.

He is a melodrama version of the self-deceiving hypocrite. That is another reason why Hawthorne holds off on explicitly labeling him a hypocrite until after he is dead. All through the novel, every time we meet the Judge (or those of his ancestors who are also his previous incarnations), he is looking hypocritical while doing hypocritical things in a hypocritical manner, and yet the words *hypocrite* and *hypocritical* are stubbornly held in reserve. If I am correct in thinking this an authorial stratagem, then it must have been decided on at a preliminary stage in the conception of the book, since the manuscript collations appended to the Centenary Edition indicate no earlier appearances of the word that were canceled. Presumably Hawthorne has all along been saving it to maximize the melodramatic impact in the finale of the climactic "Governor Pyncheon" chapter, when at last the word explodes with dactylic dissonance at the end of a string of raucous iambs—"thou subtil, worldly, selfish, iron-hearted hypocrite" (p. 283). The words are instantly repeated in full, like twin bursts from a battery of ack-ack guns. Of course, the noise is insufficient to arouse the would-be governor, and this is part of Hawthorne's intention: to suggest that the nature of Judge Pyncheon's hypocrisy and the essence of his entire character are such as to make him equally impervious to the word alive or dead.

Most critics since Henry James have noticed two things about Judge Pyncheon. First, that he is a hypocrite—"a superb, full-blown hypocrite," writes James, "a large-based, full-nurtured Pharisee, bland, urbane, impressive, diffusing about him a 'sultry' warmth of benevolence . . . and basking in the noontide of prosperity and the consideration of society; but in reality hard, gross, and ignoble." The second thing everyone notices about the Judge is that Hawthorne did not especially succeed in realizing him fully—to James, again, he is "a picture rather than a character" and, "in spite of the space he occupies an accessory figure."[13] I quite agree, but I would be more particular and call the Judge a caricature of a hypocrite, especially of the self-deceiving hypocrites described by some of the old Puritan hypocrite-hunters we discussed earlier. For instance, he shares many character traits with John Cotton's goats. Unlike the transparently hypocritical swine, we recall, the self-deceiving goats reveal their hypocrisy through their over-zealousness for purity: they are "full of Ambition, they cannot abide the swamps and holes, but will be climbing upon the tops of mountains." Judge Pyncheon leads an exemplary life outwardly, filled with prayers, Bible societies, and philanthropic enterprises, and he sees no contradiction, or even distinction, between such activities and his unremitting efforts to augment his personal wealth and power. He is also like a Cotton goat in terms of his characteristics as an individual—although, since both caricatures are devised largely for satiric purposes, neither is much individu-alized. However, what Cotton says of his goat applies equally to Hawthorne's Judge, who, like the goat, "affecteth Eminency, his gate also is stately." We may also presume that the Judge par-ticularly resembles the "old Goats" in being a "Rankish" creature with an "unsavory relish"—this would provide a further explana-tion for Phoebe's unthinking recoil from his attempted embrace.

Speaking of that intended kiss, the explanation Hawthorne offers for its failure to connect brings up another aspect of the Judge's personality that derives not so much from Puritan thought on hypocrisy as from old stereotypes in sectarian polemics, such as in certain seventeenth-century character sketches, about the hy-pocrisy of Puritans. At first we are told that the Judge seeks the kiss "with the pardonable and even praiseworthy purpose—consider-ing the nearness of blood and the difference of age—" of express-ing an avuncular, familial, and "natural affection." No doubt this is what the Judge thinks he is doing. But from Phoebe's perspective the approaching gesture of affection seems less natural, or at least not so innocent. While the Judge's physical presence at a safe distance "might not be absolutely unpleasant to the feminine beholder"—perhaps the experience might even be a pleasant one to feminine beholders who agree with Henry Kissinger that power is an aphrodisiac—"it became too intense, when this dark, full-fed physiognomy (so roughly bearded, too, that no razor could ever make it smooth) sought to bring itself into actual contact with the object of its regards." The innuendo of sexual exploitation is brought out by the reification of language—he is an "it" and she is an "object of its regards"—and reinforced by the imagery of rough, hirsute masculinity. "The man, the sex, somehow or other, was 101 entirely too prominent," the description continues, less obliquely, and it is no wonder Phoebe "felt herself blushing deeply under his look" (p. 118).

An old goat in every sense of the word, the Judge embodies the carnality that the Puritans were often charged with maintaining beneath a mask of asceticism.[14] Although he had thoroughly "reformed" following "a dissipated youth" (p. 23), the appetites that led him into dissipation apparently have continued to exert influence on him. Such had also been the case with his ancestor the Colonel, who "had fallen into transgressions to which men of his great animal developement, whatever their faith or principles, must continue liable" (p. 122). Presumably the manifestations of the Judge's erotic drives have been, like his grab for Phoebe, less readily identifiable as "transgressions" than were the unspecified lapses of the Colonel, just as his capacity to exhaust bed partners has been only a third that of his ancestor, who "had worn out three wives, and merely by the remorseless weight of his character in the conjugal relation" (p. 123). The Judge's transgressions, then, are less weighty and therefore more easily overlooked. Crews writes that "it is suggested more than once" that the Judge has actually transgressed just like the Colonel, but he doesn't reveal the location of these suggestions.[15] I suppose one would be the statement, occurring in the paragraph before the comparison between the two men's married lives, that "there were traditions about the ancestor, and private diurnal gossip about the Judge, remarkably accordant in their testimony" (p. 122). However, this remark occurs in the context of a long "parallel" drawn between the two in which a balance is insisted upon between "hereditary resemblances" and a long process of family degeneration, particularly in "the necessity for animal force" (pp. 123, 121). So when particular misdeeds are contrasted, the Colonel's transgressions should be thought of as physical, completely willful and unambiguous: he wears out three wives. On the other hand, the "gossip" about the Judge is in the same "tradition" but involves less "animal force." He wears his one wife out by abusing her psychologically; specifically, he makes her serve him coffee in bed on their honeymoon (p. 123).

The point here is that it is a selling-short of Hawthorne's skill at subtly delineating a character, even a satiric caricature, to think of the Judge as merely a watered-down version of the Colonel, or, to take Hawthorne's own metaphor, an exact replica of the Colonel except underweight by fifty-six pounds (p. 121). Metaphors should be understood metaphorically, not literally. It won't do simply to leave it where Gray leaves it: "The Judge is much smoother than the Colonel, a suave hypocrite rather than simply and roughly two-faced."[16] It should be borne in mind how perplexing a problem it is for Holgrave to establish which of the Judge's two faces is his real face. In referring to the Judge as a caricature of a hypocrite, I didn't mean that he is a simple caricature. Several critics have demonstrated an awareness of the complexity of the picture but have not gone far out of their way to explain it. The sticky part comes when they try to determine the Judge's motives or intentions. Newton Arvin, to begin with, finds it "instructive" to examine the rendering of Judge Pyncheon, "Hawthorne's only elaborate study of the hypocrite"; however, in summarizing what it is that makes the Judge so hypocritical, Arvin is constrained to resort to some curious weasel-wording of his own. Thus the young future jurist doesn't lie outright when he incriminates young Clifford; rather, "he does not scruple to take upon his conscience an inactive falsehood." Nor does he set out to destroy his wife and son; instead, they "go down before the hardness and harshness of his will." Arvin can't even say that the Judge willfully pursues selfish ends. It is the other way around: he is "dominated" by a "self-seeking purpose" which he more or less passively "allows . . . to triumph over every humane consideration."[17]

The tortured language arises from Arvin's unspoken realization that a more straightforward account would not be accurate. He avoids coming to grips with the disparity by effectively throwing up his hands and formulaically declaring that for Judge Pyncheon "the very principle of his existence" is "false." What this false principle may be is never clarified, though Arvin concludes his consideration of the Judge by remarking "the unreality of his whole life,"[18] thereby anticipating the approach of subsequent criticism that has emphasized mental abnormality over moral turpitude. Roy R. Male, for instance, attributes Judge Pyncheon's peculiarities to a subconscious "obsession" that "is never made explicit" (by either Hawthorne or Male) and to misapprehensions of reality in general and particularly to those with regard to time. This way Male is automatically spared Arvin's difficulties regarding the Judge's smiling villainy. For Male, the Judge remains complacently unaware of the tangle of evil within him simply because his perceptive faculties do not function adequately: "On the surface (and this, of course, is as far as his self-analysis would go), his motives are clear."[19] Only these aren't his real motives; those motives remain hidden, much as external reality remains largely inaccessible to his understanding. In a similar manner Crews observes that Judge Pyncheon's "villainy is separated from his conscience by layers of self-esteem and public honor," making him "an imminent presence, an unspecified threat, rather than an active criminal."[20] His criminality is not "active," we might assume, because it is "separated" from consciousness as well as from conscience, although this would be difficult to accept if it were true, as Crews also asserts, that the Judge were as calculating a malefactor as the Colonel.

It is a tribute to Hawthorne's skill that he can keep the critics guessing about the motives of a satirically drawn character whose unmistakable melodramatic villainy is made plain from the start. Hawthorne both enhances his artistic triumph and exults in it by his vocal and repeated insistence that he too just can't figure out his character's motivation or the motives of some of his only slightly differentiated ancestors. Thus, speaking of the Pyncheon clan generically, "the writer" says he "cherishes the belief that many, if not most" of them "were troubled with doubts as to their moral right" to continue to possess the property their eponymous ancestor had coveted and stolen but that even such a mild and reasonable supposition can be backed up only by "impressions often too vaguely founded to be put on paper." By the same token, the rather elementary deduction that the Pyncheons are guilty of being "conscious of wrong, and failing to rectify it" must remain no more certain than an "awful query" (p. 20). The element of doubt is consistently maintained throughout the novel, from one Pyncheon generation to the next. While the narrator wavers not at all in suggesting that nothing but greed lay in back of the Colonel's original crime against Matthew Maule, he can't decide whether the victim's son was later awarded the building contract because "the Colonel thought it expedient, or was impelled by some better feeling, thus openly to cast aside all animosity against the race of his fallen antagonist" (p. 10). It is also left up in the air whether in the following century another Pyncheon turned his coat back from tory to patriot because he really repented or because he too thought it expedient to avoid confiscation of his house (p. 22). Yet another, the one Clifford was supposed to have murdered, may actually have intended belatedly "substituting right for wrong," or at least such "was the belief of those who knew him best" (whoever they might have been, since we're also told several times that he was an "old bachelor" who lived a "secluded" life). But, alas, even posthumously the deed proved "too powerful" for his "conscientious scruples" (p. 23). Alice Pyncheon's Europeanized father had his "scruples" too, but again, the narrator (Holgrave, actually) points out in passing that it is not known precisely why he momentarily hesitated to sacrifice his daughter for selfish ends—whether out of "conscience, pride, or fatherly affection" (p. 200). The reader must choose.

The uncertainty surrounding the Pyncheons' motivation is most insistent with regard to the Judge. "His motives and intentions . . . are a mystery to me," confesses Holgrave (p. 217), functioning here, I think, as he so often does in many different ways throughout the book, as an authorial mouthpiece. The author himself never expresses his bewilderment quite so directly, although in the next chapter he just as effectively reveals his almost private sense of the inner mysteriousness of this character who, as he would know better than anyone, must have struck his readers from the first as a most blatant beast. Yet Hawthorne exhorts us (not entirely in jest) to do his villainous jurist the "justice" to recognize that "probably" the Judge didn't "entertain many or very frequent doubts" that he truly was every bit as virtuous as he appeared to be (p. 228). These rare doubts, of course, are well-founded: there lurks deep within his soul something "evil and unsightly" which is both "hidden from mankind" and "forgotten by himself." In the original manuscript Hawthorne evidently had written "hidden from himself," then changed it to the present reading, perceiving, we may surmise, the perplexing consequences of the earlier version. Hidden from himself by whom? Could he ever have found it? As it stands, the issue is all but hopelessly snarled, as we are asked to "venture" that a man's "guilt" might be a "daily" feature of his life "without his necessarily, and at every moment, being aware of it" (p. 229). No wonder Hawthorne, as if realizing that his speculative "venture" is carrying him far afield into areas not really essential to the needs of the story he is telling at the moment, beats a wise and hasty retreat back into the artistry of his novel—specifically into the elaborately contrived set-piece metaphor wherein the Judge's 105 character is compared to an elaborately laid-out (and presumably seven-gabled) house. But the "pool of stagnant water" underlying the analogical house is situated with far greater precision (and is much less murky) than what it purports to contain: the secret of "this man's miserable soul" (p. 230). A franker appraisal of the limitations Hawthorne has come up against occurs at the end of the chapter when, about to kill the man off, he admits between dashes that "we know not the secret of his heart." And then, as if he had grown as weary of juggling his character's uncertain motives as the Judge himself seems to have grown of his self-deceiving life, he allows Hepzibah, who up to now has been the only one never in doubt as to her cousin's malign intentions, to hear an "imagined" utterance from the Judge, "which she was anxious to interpret as a relenting impulse" (p. 238). The "awful query" raised at the outset concerning consciousness of wrong in the hypocritical Pyncheon clan remains unanswered to the end.

Aside from Fogle, who in passing calls him "a hypocrite, himself deceived,"[21] there would appear to be little awareness by critics of, or interest in, the element of self-deception in Judge Pyncheon's hypocrisy. Yet to me it is too prominent to deny and too important to overlook. When he assures Hepzibah that Clifford will find "love enough" in his eye, we are told that he says this with "well-grounded confidence in the benignity of his aspect" (p. 233). It seems to me that we can account for his confidence in his loving appearance being well grounded, not by thinking of him as a pantomimist of consummate skill, and not by assuming that Hawthorne is merely trying to be funny, but only by conceding that the Judge really does believe in his benignity, although of course he couldn't be more mistaken.

Moreover, I would suggest that Hawthorne's portrait of Judge Pyncheon can be traced more directly than might his other characterizations to the Puritan conception of self-deceiving hypocrisy from which, I contend, his overall approach ultimately derives. Aside from the resemblances already noted to John Cotton's rankish old goats, there are also specific aspects of the treatment of hypocrites in deeper works, such as Thomas Shepard's *Parable of the Ten Virgins*, that closely correspond to Hawthorne's depiction of the Judge. For one thing, Shepard emphasizes the special affinity for hypocrites of the last of the deadly sins: "that Spirit of sloath and slumber, which the Lord ever leaves the best Hypocrite unto;

which is the dearest lust and last enemy that the Lord destroyes in all his, but never destroies in these." It is their sloth and not their hypocrisy per se that proves the means of their undoing: "When the swine have no swill to eat, yet you shall find them in the mire of sloath; this *slaies the foolish.*"[22] Similarly, Hawthorne tells us early on that in the Pyncheon family line, the "baser sort" have long displayed a "liability to sluggishness and dependence," exacerbated by their dreams of unearned wealth (p. 19). Regardless of his achievements and ambitions, Judge Pyncheon evidently belongs to this sort, at least insofar as his physical appearance and carriage may be taken as emblematic of the man. We first see him "passing slowly along" the street, and even his clothes have "a wide and rich gravity about them" (reminiscent, perhaps, of the gilded leaden cloaks worn by the hypocrites in Canto 23 of the *Inferno*), while his heavy cane, were it capable of locomotion, would "walk" much as he does (p. 56). Hawthorne provides another exhibition of his skill at sloth-related synecdoche when on a subsequent visit to the seven-gabled house we hear the Judge's foot "scraping itself on the threshold, and thence somewhat ponderously stepping on the floor"; whereupon we next hear a "characteristic sound, . . . neither a cough nor a hem, but a kind of rumbling and reverberating spasm in somebody's capacious depth of chest" (p. 225), as though he lacks the energy even to clear his throat effectively. Naturally, his slothfulness is further magnified by his death. Clifford and Hepzibah leave him sitting "heavy and lumpish" (p. 252). And later the sarcastic narrator wonders about "the unaccountable lethargy, which . . . has made him such a laggard" (p. 273)—echoing his earlier puzzlement over the "sluggishness on Colonel Pyncheon's part" that was delaying the appearance of the Judge's seventeenth-century avatar at the housewarming (p. 13). The sloth motif climaxes immediately after the (defunct) Judge is at last called a hypocrite, at which point a fly lights on his nose and Hawthorne snidely remarks, "Canst thou not brush the fly away? Art thou too sluggish?" (p. 283). In Shepard's phrasing, this slays the foolish.

The very savagery with which the narrator taunts the Judge's corpse has its counterpart in the *Parable* and may well be attributable to Hawthorne's sharing with Shepard a private horror at the thought of being somehow self-deceived. Hawthorne's readers are asked if the Judge will "go forth a humbled and repentant man"

(p. 282), a question that is terrifying in its context precisely because it need not be answered—we well understand that it is no longer possible for him to escape damnation. More explicitly chilling is Shepard's grim assurance to his readers that "the portion of Hypocrites" is to find themselves with "poor hearts, eyes dim, hearts hard, Consciences asleep, ears deaf, breath gone, life lost, God departed, and nothing left but a dead Carcase."[23]

The unremitting ferocity with which the Judge is damned leads me to categorize *The House of the Seven Gables*, despite its self-consciously comedic resolution, as Hawthorne's most narrowly Calvinistic novel in its treatment of the crucial issue of salvation and damnation. Unlike *The Scarlet Letter*, which might at first glance seem a more appropriate candidate for the distinction, there is no troubling doctrinal ambivalence at the end of the story. Dimmesdale may or may not find peace and forgiveness on the scaffold, but Alice Pyncheon flies to heaven, all too literally, while the Judge is grotesquely damned, just like the good and bad little girls and boys in storybooks for Puritan children. It is Calvinism with a vengeance, so to speak.

That is not to say, however, that Hawthorne wrote the book as a vehicle for Calvinist theology. On the contrary, if I am correct in calling *The House of the Seven Gables* his most narrowly Calvinistic novel, that would only tend to confirm our usual impression of his reluctance to make theological commitments of any kind, and particularly to Calvinist doctrines, because the overall tone of the book is so melodramatic and gothic on the one hand, and so satirical and almost tongue-in-cheek on the other, that we can hardly suppose the author means us to take the theology he exploits for artistic purposes as what he actually believes or wants us to believe. Hawthorne is no Calvinist, but he feels no reluctance toward using elements of Calvinist theology for ends that are literary. Calvinism provides him with a means of further developing one of his greatest themes: the nature of hypocrisy and self-deception and their relation to morality. The Puritans' preoccupation with hypocrisy is an important part of the historical development of the theme within Western culture, and in this novel Hawthorne's entire treatment of the problem, at least with regard to the characterization of the Judge, seems dominated by a Calvinistic outlook that closely parallels colonial points of view. His treatment of similar issues elsewhere, even in *The Scarlet Letter,* is less narrowly "theological" in this sense.

There are, of course, other aspects to Judge Pyncheon's hypocrisy besides the religious. The political dimension is briefly yet expansively analyzed in a segment of Judith Shklar's article "Let Us Not Be Hypocritical": Shklar relates Judge Pyncheon's hypocrisy to a characteristic strain in American politics epitomized, though in a rather more positive sense, by Benjamin Franklin.[24] Hawthorne may have been aided in blending the religious and political aspects by one of his possible sources for the novel, William Cobbett's *Sermons on Hypocrisy and Cruelty,* which he charged from the Salem Athenaeum in 1828.[25] Cobbett, an English peasant-radical and onetime pamphleteer for the American Federalists, was much admired by Hawthorne, who once referred to him as a "true blood hound of literature."[26] Although a professed Anglican, Cobbett was mainly secular in outlook and political in his interests, and it is likely that he called his pamphlets "sermons" merely to circumvent British censorship.[27] Nonetheless, there are strong religious elements in his political attacks against hypocrisy, which for Cobbett generally meant the preaching of religion as an insidious means of maintaining the repression of the poor.[28]

The possible influence of Cobbett's book appears in two significant ways. First, one of his "sermons" concerns the biblical story of Naboth's vineyard, which may underlie the plot of Hawthorne's romance.[29] In Cobbett's version, the wealthy coveter of his poor neighbor's property is a religious hypocrite who "will proceed to almost any lengths" to get what he wants; like Colonel Pyncheon he uses "false swearings" and "will, without the least remorse, dip his hands in the blood of the innocent." Another "sermon," entitled "God's Judgment on Unjust Judges," presents a description similarly reminiscent of Judge Pyncheon:

> Hypocrisy, always odious, is never quite so odious as when employed as a mask for judicial injustice: it is the garb of piety assumed for the purpose of committing cruelty; the garb of religion put on in order to sanctify a violation of all the laws of God and man. Against the petulant, the intemperate, the violent, the openly profligate perverter of judgment, the oppressed usually find some remedy, some means of arresting the progress

of his iniquity: but, against the perversion of judgment by the
cool, placid, deep-designing religious hypocrite, there is no
redress other than that afforded by the interposition of the
Almighty.[30]

It is indeed the Almighty who, when all hope seems lost, provides
a swift and terrible redress for wrongs perpetrated by the hypocritical judge in *The House of the Seven Gables*. To Cobbett, however, feigned religiosity is merely part of the hypocrite's method
for obtaining worldly ends, whereas it is in his religiosity above all
that Judge Pyncheon's hypocrisy resides. Certainly there are other
dimensions to his hypocrisy, but it is as a religious hypocrite that
he most clearly reveals his essence and merits his damnation.

He is a self-deceived hypocrite, and his portrait is drawn more or
less after the manner of the old Puritan hypocrite-hunters. They
well understood how hypocrites by their every word and deed
might seem models of devout Christians and yet be, as Hooker
describes his "glorious" hypocrites, "wens in the profession of the
Gospel" who "never had the Spirit of Christ powerfully prevailing
with them."[31] Moreover, the depths of their evil nature may ex-
tend precisely from the core of their seeming piety: in Willard's
formulation, "a man may fail in his duty, and be guilty before God
of sinning against him, in the very action wherein he keeps most
close to the letter of the law."[32] His having come howsoever "close"
to righteousness in no way mitigates his sin; rather, it damns him all
the more for profaning holy things.

Most of what we learn of the Pyncheon reputation for Christian
probity comes heavily spiked with patent sarcasm, as when an
obsequious Puritan clergyman eulogizes Colonel Pyncheon as a
saint in heaven (pp. 17, 121), or a partisan newspaper prints an
encomium of the Judge for his "display of every grace and virtue . . . befitting the christian, the good citizen, the horticulturist,
and the gentleman!" (p. 24). As might be expected, the undercut-
ting is more subtly accomplished when it derives directly from the
narrator without intermediary. Thus right after the cesspool metaphor Hawthorne enumerates items of conscience-paralyzing "rubbish" in Judge Pyncheon's life, among them "his remarkable zeal
as president of a Bible society" and "his prayers at morning and
eventide, and graces at mealtime." He is moved by this inventory
to inquire, "What is there so ponderous in evil, that a thumb's

bigness of it should outweigh the mass of things not evil, which were heaped into the other scale!" (pp. 230, 231). What "people of Judge Pyncheon's brotherhood"—meaning, of course, hypocrites—fail to realize, Hawthorne proposes in answer to this question, is that all this "mass of things," even if not actually evil, are assuredly not any good either. At best they are "rubbish"—of no weight or value. Their apparent bulk is attributable to pernicious, ultimately fatal self-deception. Interestingly, Hawthorne speculates that the only hope left for such people to acquire "true self-knowledge" lies through severe affliction—"loss of property," disease, the approach of death (p. 232)—as if hypocrites were in some odd way like a tribe of failed Jobs.

Denied the possibility of cure through suffering, the Judge unwittingly is abandoned to the terrible situation of an utter lack of moral awareness. So profound is his self-deception that he has no inkling that the "free and christianlike forgiveness" expressed in his "countenance" for his virtually face-slapping adversary, Hepzibah (p. 232), is as eschatologically worthless to him as his Bible society and his twice-daily prayers. This is Hawthorne's dreadful judgment on the Judge's strongest attempt to justify himself as he pleads with Hepzibah for an interview with Clifford, his "impressive earnestness of manner" approaching "tearful pathos." His every action the Judge attributes to "duty and conscience"; the advantages that provide the power he wields over others he calls "the prosperity with which Heaven has blessed me"; his character he proclaims to be "true, to the heart's core" (p. 227). Indeed he protests too much, but not from lack of conviction. On the contrary, it is through the very totality of his conviction that Hawthorne is able to show how irreclaimably rotten to the core his heart really is.

It would be a mistake to regard him as simply an updated Tartuffe or Onuphre, cynically feigning a piety he does not feel in order to forward his selfish interests. Such a reading would reduce the entire novel to the shallowness to which it now deteriorates only at the end. Judge Pyncheon's piety is a false piety, but he believes it to be true; yet however "sincere" his belief, the falseness remains undiminished. Writing this way is difficult, and we can still see traces of the difficulties Hawthorne encountered in describing such a character by examining the record of alterations in his manuscript, as catalogued by the editors of the Centenary Edition, particularly in the chapter called "The Scowl and Smile." 111

The chapter is crucial to establishing the reader's appreciation of the intricate psychological framework in which the characters function. As it proceeds we realize that even the simple title carries nuances and ambiguities: it may refer to Hepzibah's outer scowl and inner compassion, or the Judge's outer smile and inner pitilessness. We might recall that Chillingworth, another deadly hypocrite, is at one point said to resemble "the arch-fiend, standing there, with a smile and scowl, to claim his own" (1:156).

The structure of the chapter is complex, with a long exposition concerning the Judge's character interrupting the dramatic confrontation at a critical point, like a flashback inserted between freeze frames in a movie. The writing is correspondingly dense and, judging from manuscript evidence, heavily worked over. One alteration, emending "hidden from himself" to something less enigmatic, I have already commented on. Another, occurring at the critical freeze-frame instant, looks awkward in the published text. Hepzibah threatens to "spurn at" the Judge (p. 228), Hawthorne having decided to soften "spit at" to "spurn" but failing to cancel the "at," perhaps from an unconscious reluctance to tone down her just indignation at her enemy's heartlessness. Other changes are more calculated and so easier to analyze, and from their cumulative effect they add to the conception of the Judge as a self-deceiving hypocrite. Thus he tells Hepzibah that he is glad Clifford's release is "deemed consistent with the dues of public justice and the welfare of society" (p. 227), with the word *public* interlined so the Judge won't seem to be admitting inadvertently that his cousin's freedom might be even more consistent with some higher concept of justice. After Hepzibah's outburst, the long, interrupting exposition begins with a comment on her "unconquerable distrust of Judge Pyncheon's integrity." Here, *integrity* has been substituted for the original *character* mainly for stylistic reasons: so as not to repeat that word in asking whether her distrust should be attributed to "any just perception of his character" or to "a woman's unreasoning prejudice"—with *unreasoning* interlined (p. 228). But the stylistic alteration, as well as the addition of *unreasoning*, also sharpens the argument greatly. The answer to the question is that both attributions for Hepzibah's distrust for the Judge are correct when taken together: the truth of his character can be justly perceived only by those who trust their irrational emotions, since the reasoning people who comprise society at large perceive him falsely and mistakenly trust his integrity. His hypocrisy is impenetrable by rational observation, including the Judge's own, because there are no outward signs of it that are revealed to the characters in the novel, though they are, of course, plentifully exhibited to the reader, in the same way that only the reader knows from outward signs about Hepzibah's inner goodness. Even a trivial change such as altering the extent to which the Judge has cut down on his sherry drinking—at first Hawthorne had him reduce it to two glasses a day then altered *two* to *five* in the manuscript (p. 231)—demonstrates how subtly Hawthorne avoids sending clear signals to his characters about the truth of their own situations. Had the glasses of sherry been cut down to only two, the Judge could have unobjectionably congratulated himself on his judicial sobriety; yet had he only been allowed to succeed in restricting himself to no fewer than, say, seven, he might have become concerned he was drifting into alcoholism. Five is right on the borderline. With this, as with more important matters, the truth about the Judge is accessible through reason only to those outside the book; those inside either "know" through nonrational means (Hepzibah, Phoebe) or become dupes of his hypocrisy, as he becomes the dupe of his own self-deception.

By two final alterations Hawthorne manages to avoid the risk of having the reader miss the point entirely through excessive indirection, and yet he also avoids falling into the opposite fault of tendentious overstatement. First, in the hidden cesspool analogy, he added the explicit admission that the inhabitant of the ill-smelling house "will not be conscious of it" (p. 230). Even more pointedly, as the expository section ends and the action is about to resume, Hawthorne originally summed up the Judge's character by describing him as "resolutely taking his idea of himself from his image, as reflected in the mirror of public opinion," but changed the first part of this to "what purports to be his image" (p. 232). The clarification again brings up the problematic issue surrounding Holgrave's daguerreotypes and what constitutes a true likeness. The Judge is resolved to accept his appearance as his essence. The joke is that ultimately he is correct in doing so: once he is dead his purported image changes, both physically and by reputation, and becomes congruent with his true identity.

The true identity can be seen only in retrospect, or, as Thomas   113

Shepard might have preferred to say, when there is "nothing left but a dead Carcase." As with the portrait of Colonel Pyncheon, "the unlovely truth of a human soul" arrives at the surface only "after the superficial coloring has been rubbed off by time" (p. 59), although it appears that photography greatly accelerates the process. What that unlovely truth actually is—which is to say, what does it really mean to be damned?—is difficult to determine, regardless of one's theological convictions or lack of them. Phoebe, with her enhanced sensitivity, takes a sidelong glance at the Pyncheon ugliness and perceives it as in some way "hereditary." On one level, "hereditary" merely recasts predestination into terms acceptable to a more enlightened age, in a manner similar to what Emerson is sometimes capable of doing with a word like "temperament." Throughout the nineteenth century, heredity often carried the sense of a force that antedates yet fatally underlies any individual existence—one thinks of the determination of character by heredity in Ibsen. But Hawthorne may have been reaching beyond a commonplace biological determinism. "A deeper philosopher than Phoebe," he comments on the not especially deep reference to heredity, "might have found something very terrible in this idea" (p. 119). The tacit acknowledgment here of Hawthorne's own philosophical shortcomings, even if we take it at face value (though Hawthorne certainly isn't a Phoebe!), shouldn't mislead us into discounting the more profound implications in his work that he seems to be directing our attention to, almost personally.

That the very terrible idea of a man's ineluctable destruction is applied to an emphatically nontragic character like Judge Pyncheon is no real incongruity in the wider context of the novel. True, the Judge is in large measure made to serve as the butt of satire, and we are most certainly meant to laugh at his undoing. However, the satire is of the biting rather than the gentle variety, and our laughter has some savagery in it—we laugh as the audience at a medieval morality play might have laughed while watching a sinner, shrieking and pleading, being dragged off to hell by sadistic demons. Hawthorne succinctly combines the two sides of the apparent contradiction when, near the beginning of the "Governor Pyncheon" chapter, he describes himself as either "enemy or mischief-maker," gazing into the dead man's "wide-open eyes," in order to "peep through these windows into his consciousness, and make strange discoveries" (p. 269)—which, as the chapter unfolds, is precisely what he does in a manner that is at once both elfishly mischievous and scornfully hostile.

By making himself an "enemy or mischief-maker," Hawthorne is assuming the role of death as the revealer of hidden truth. The gravestone carver Wigglesworth performs the same moral function in "Chippings with a Chisel," but this time Hawthorne acts not through a proxy but directly, as self-conscious narrator and literary artist. In this respect he anticipates his next romance, in which an artist-character as narrator attempts to confront and transcend hypocrisy and self-deception in himself and in life generally by means of the narrative itself. But as we shall see, in that work the emphasis in the final analysis shifts away decidedly from the moral issues it raises to the ontological question—what is the real self?—which in turn becomes subsumed into the larger problems of the relations between illusion and reality and between art and life.

His interest in hypocrisy and self-deception in and of themselves is obviously waning in *The House of the Seven Gables*, most evidently in the cavalier manner with which both moral and ontological issues are perfunctorily dismissed at the end:

> Thus, Jaffrey Pyncheon's inward criminality, as regarded Clifford, was indeed black and damnable; while its mere outward show and positive commission was the smallest that could possibly consist with so great a sin. This is just the sort of guilt that a man of eminent respectability finds it easiest to dispose of. It was suffered to fade out of sight, or be reckoned a venial matter, in the Honorable Judge Pyncheon's long subsequent survey of his own life. He shuffled it aside, among the forgotten and forgiven frailties of his youth, and seldom thought of it again. (p. 312)

We can accept his having "shuffled aside" memories of a robbery, a lurid death, and perjury only as a means of allowing the author to bring his romance to a hasty conclusion. Certainly, given the nature of this story, there would have been no point in carrying out his investigation of the paradox of self-deception as far as he had in *The Scarlet Letter*, and perhaps his lack of seriousness at the end might best be regarded as an expression of his having put behind him any lingering urges to resolve the unresolvable. Yet enough of the mystery remains that we cannot rest satisfied with the cursory treatment it receives at the end of *The House of the Seven Gables*. It is not enough to think: well, this is merely melodrama and satire. There is also a more than vestigial sense of awe and even of terror, and though they are not fully realized, they will not go away and cannot be "shuffled aside."

SIX

The Blithedale Romance: "The Dust of Deluded Generations"

In the broad pattern of Hawthorne's fiction, death and art are allies in the effort to penetrate a given character's hypocrisies and self-deceptions and to reveal the inner truth, both morally with regard to the state of a character's soul and ontologically with regard to the core of a character's identity. Like a daguerrotyper exposing the secrets of a face to the sunlight, or a stone carver shaping and inscribing a frozen monument to a now unalterable life, death fixes on a man his final and permanent image, the image that remains with us as we finish reading the story. But in turning from the comparatively simple last glimpses of Goodman Brown in despair of humanity or of Ethan Brand in despair of God to the many-layered mystery of Dimmesdale on the scaffold, we sense a slight shift of emphasis from morality to ontology, and from the revelatory power of death to the imaging power of art. We know that the inner truth of Dimmesdale's life is there on the scaffold for all to see, revealed by a sign, but we do not know what the sign is because *we* never actually see it, either literally or figuratively. For once, everyone else—all the other characters—sees what we do not, rather than the other way round, and that is because, as we now realize, we have never been seeing at all. We have not been seeing but reading, and the verbal description of Dimmesdale we read at the end is no different, no less truthful, than a verbal description of Dimmesdale we might read anywhere in the book. The words reveal no more nor less the inner truth of Dimmesdale's fictional life than they reveal the inner truth of any other life, fictional or not fictional. In art as in life, there is ultimately no telling the hypocrite

117

from the saint, and no one ever knows which of the faces one wears is true.

Not even the artist, the creator, can pretend to know, but only to reveal. As we recall from the death-revelation in "Governor Pyncheon," the narrator who enters in at the dead man's eyes to proclaim him a hypocrite describes himself as an enemy, and indeed he is an enemy in the deepest sense, for it is his narration that has created the fictive world in which he decrees the dead man's damnation. But in a fictional world in which virtually everyone is in bad faith, how can the author, whose vision created that world and whose narrative sustains it, confide in his own integrity or even apprehend his own identity? I believe this is the question that resides at the thematic center of *The Blithedale Romance*. To some extent it is a formal question, but the issues it raises go beyond, in profundity as well as in complexity, familiar matters such as the so-called reliability of the narrator or the subversion of literary conventions, Furthermore, I feel that the profundity and complexity of these issues can best be appreciated by approaching the book from within the context of Hawthorne's preoccupation with hypocrisy and self-deception.

I can illustrate the relevance of our previous discussion of hypocrites and self-deceivers in the earlier fiction to this new problem in *The Blithedale Romance* of the narrator/author's integrity and identity by calling attention to a peculiar and subtle feature in the way the story is told. As before, there are final revelations of each major character's true inner state, and in one case it is also a death-revelation. Yet this time, early in the story each character effectively foretells his or her own destiny without being aware of it. Moreover, they do so the very first time they are all in one another's presence. Thus Zenobia, "shivering playfully," tells Coverdale that she won't wear the "garb of Eden" until after May Day (3:17), and indeed it is September when a Fates-like trio of old "tire-women" strip the sodden clothes off her drowned corpse (p. 237). Priscilla, similarly, arrives begging shelter and companionship, while Hollingsworth warns the women about not letting their hearts grow cold (pp. 28–29), and so when Coverdale last sees them, Priscilla has a constant companion in Hollingsworth, who in turn clings "close, and closer still" to her side (p. 242), drawing vital warmth from the one female heart that still burns for him.

At first glance Coverdale's prediction for himself seems less accurate. He shares with Zenobia his hope to write some really worthwhile poetry (p. 14), but at the end he declares his life has amounted to "Nothing, nothing, nothing!" (p. 245). Yet if at that point we reflect on the value of the narrative we have nearly finished reading, with its poetic touches such as the implausible but affecting quasi precognitions I have been referring to, we might well say that his prediction, too, has been fulfilled, since he of course is the purported author of that very narrative.

But what if we further reflect on those affecting quasi precognitions, including the one that Coverdale will become a good rather than a mediocre poet. We might ask ourselves what we are to make of their implausibility. We could then simply say that the poetic fulfillment of chance utterances is a romantic convention. But then how do we assess the cogency, if not the veracity, of Coverdale's narration, insofar as there is no overt hint that he is aware that what he writes as fact is implausible outside romantic conventions? Another possible move would be to suggest that he deliberately exploits those conventions, but that would be difficult to make sense of: it would force us to change radically our understanding of the nature of the narrative we are implicitly asked to think of him as writing.

These unsettling problems arise because Coverdale is both narrator and major character, and yet I would contend that here they are more acute than in other novels similar in that respect because Hawthorne is still operating along the lines of his earlier investigations of hypocrisy and self-deception. His interests have expanded to take him into areas where he might fairly well leave hypocrisy and self-deception behind him, and eventually he will. But first he takes a final look at his world of hypocrites and self-deceivers, this time, however, directly through the eyes of one who also lives among them. The question of Coverdale's bad faith in the final analysis is transformed into the larger question of the nature of art and its relation to life.

That the world Coverdale describes is as pervaded by hypocrisy and self-deception as in any Hawthornian setting has been noted in the criticism. Canaday, for example, condemns the "play-acting" that goes on at the commune as "a parody of the lives of real farmers," even though none of the idealists "seems even slightly aware of the patronizing attitudes displayed by each and all."[1] Coverdale, however, attributes the hostile feelings of the local   119 farmers toward the commune not to understandable resentment over being parodied and patronized but rather to "pure envy and malice" (p. 65), and in fact the only character to explicitly dismiss the commune as a pretentious sham is the sneering hypocrite Westervelt (p. 91). Contradicting both Canaday and Westervelt, Coverdale asserts that the communards took unreservedly to "yeoman-life" (p. 64) and demonstrates their success in adapting to it by contrasting the inability of visitors to keep pace with them when they are at their chores (pp. 81–82).

What is significant here is not whether Blithedale is a sham (in some sense it obviously is) nor whether the envious neighbors are hypocrites (no doubt to some degree they are) but rather the explicit awareness of this by a central character and the attitude he adopts as narrator in telling us as readers. The awareness, found in no other Hawthorne character, is as acute as that of the usual Hawthornian omniscient narrator, but the attitude or tone is different. "Altogether, by projecting our minds outward, we had imparted a show of novelty to existence," he reflects on the Blithedale experiment, "and contemplated it as hopefully as if the soil, beneath our feet, had not been fathom-deep with the dust of deluded generations, on every one of which, as on ourselves, the world had imposed itself as a hitherto unwedded bride" (p. 128). The tone with which this magnificent imagery is conveyed is elegiac, despite the nihilistic content, which might be supposed to arise from a sense of despair. People deceive themselves, mistaking for reality their own mental projections, while the world they embrace as a virgin is really a whore tricked out in their own delusions. Nonetheless, though sad and regretful, Coverdale appears to understand and even seems willing to accept this state of affairs as the way things are. He, too, embraces the world, delusions and all.

Coverdale faces a world of hypocrisy and self-deception in a way that up until now we would not have expected from Hawthorne, without the righteous indignation of "The Gentle Boy," the pessimistic resignation of *The Scarlet Letter,* or the savage mockery of *The House of the Seven Gables.* The difference in his attitude can best be seen in his relationship to Hollingsworth first of all, and secondarily to Zenobia and Priscilla.

As a self-deceiving hypocrite, Hollingsworth is an even more extreme case than Judge Pyncheon's. As Baym observes, his "sheer,

if unconscious" hypocrisy is particularly unmistakable in the "disparity between his self-righteous dismissal of Zenobia and the
nature of his own motives" in throwing her over for Priscilla.[2] But
unlike the Judge, who as we recall was never given any hint from
which he might have inferred the truth about his true inner state,
Hollingsworth has every opportunity to overcome his self-deception. Indeed, Zenobia takes him step by step through an exercise
that duplicates almost exactly Herbert Fingarette's method of
"spelling-out" one's motives to avoid acting in bad faith.

First she lays out for him the bare facts of his conduct. Believing
she had money, he said he loved her, then "only three days" ago she
lost the inheritance, and she suspects he learned of this at the same
time. He doesn't deny it. Then she simply asks if he now loves
Priscilla. Hollingsworth concedes that the alteration in his affections has been sudden, and yet he declares his love for Priscilla
twice over, "uttering the words with a deep, inward breath." At
last the exasperated Zenobia tells him directly, in so many words:
"You are a better masquerader than the witches and gipsies yonder;
for your disguise is a self-deception." But it does no good; he grows
"deadly pale" but dismisses the accusation. He will not be undeceived (pp. 216–18).

Nor is it the first time anyone has tried. A hundred pages earlier
Coverdale had been attempting to persuade Hollingsworth of the
impropriety of pretending to believe in the Blithedale experiment
while secretly plotting its overthrow. He gives his friend a lecture
on how an idealist can be misled into doing wrong which is vaguely
similar to Hegel's account, in Jonathan Robinson's interpretation,
of the dutiful man's slide into hypocrisy. "At some point of his
course—I know not exactly when nor where," Coverdale explains
to Hollingsworth, "he is tempted to palter with the right, and can
scarcely forbear persuading himself that the importance of his
public ends renders it allowable to throw aside his private conscience" (p. 132). But Coverdale's attempt at reasoning is no more
effective than Zenobia's bluntness.

Coverdale had been aware of Hollingsworth's "self-delusive
egotism" (p. 79) from early on, and yet he never entirely loses faith
in the man's inner decency, even as Hollingsworth virtually does all
he can, by word and deed, to deny it. Thus when Coverdale thanks
his friend for tending him in his illness with a "tenderness" that
"seems to me the reflection of God's own love," Hollingsworth
unexpectedly retorts: "I should say rather, that the most marked

trait in my character is an inflexible severity of purpose. Mortal man has no right to be so inflexible, as it is my nature and necessity to be!" Coverdale replies, "I do not believe it," but immediately comments to the reader: "But, in due time, I remembered what he said" (p. 43). Clearly both are right. It is, unfortunately for him and for everyone around him, Hollingsworth's "nature and necessity" to act like a megalomaniacal tyrant, but in the end Coverdale's assessment is vindicated as Hollingsworth becomes a sincere penitent, even if it is after the damage has been done. The others apparently share Coverdale's charitable insight, or so we might infer from Priscilla's unshakable devotion and from Zenobia's final remarks to her false former lover, "that a great and rich heart has been ruined in your breast" (p. 219).

But only Coverdale has the intellectual equipment to attempt to understand the mechanism of self-deception and the moral complications it entails. Horrified by the suspicion that Hollingsworth's nursing of him may have been a hypocritical ploy—"only for the ulterior purpose of making me a proselyte to his views"—he sees it as a nearly pathological delusion, offering his "private opinion, that, at this period of his life, Hollingsworth was fast going mad" (pp. 57, 56). His "over-ruling purpose," which accounts for his hypocrisy, is seen as something largely external to his inner self, making him to some degree a victim of it. "He was not altogether human," writes Coverdale just before launching into a long speculation that he afterward will admit has been "exaggerated, in the attempt to make it adequate." Adequate or not, it is Hawthorne's most ambitious attempt to explicate the sort of psychological phenomenon he so masterfully illustrates. "There was something else in Hollingsworth, beside flesh and blood, and sympathies and affections, and celestial spirit," he begins. Here is the next paragraph:

> This is always true of those men who have surrendered
> themselves to an over-ruling purpose. It does not so much impel
> them from without, nor even operate as a motive power within,
> but grows incorporate with all that they think and feel, and finally
> converts them into little else save that one principle. When such
> begins to be the predicament, it is not cowardice, but wisdom, to
> avoid these victims. They have no heart, no sympathy, no reason,
> no conscience. They will keep no friend, unless he make himself

the mirror of their purpose; they will smite and slay you, and trample your dead corpse under foot, all the more readily, if you take the first step with them, and cannot take the second, and the third, and every other step of their terribly straight path. They have an idol, to which they consecrate themselves high-priest, and deem it holy work to offer sacrifices of whatever is most precious, and never once seem to suspect—so cunning has the Devil been with them—that this false deity, in whose iron features, immitigable to all the rest of mankind, they see only benignity and love, is but a spectrum of the very priest himself, projected upon the surrounding darkness. And the higher and purer the original object, and the more unselfishly it may have been taken up, the slighter is the probability that they can be led to recognize the process by which godlike benevolence has been debased into all-devouring egotism. (pp. 70–71)

Compared with the case of the Judge, whose purposes are indwelling rather than "over-ruling," Hollingsworth is in some sense a "victim" of his evil. But at the same time, his "purpose" without much difficulty "converts" him rather than being obliged to take the trouble to "impel" him, which implies that he is by no means the helpless instrument of an irresistible delusion, such as in paranoia. Most significantly, it is the "cunning" of "the Devil" to appeal, not to his base desires, but to his noble aspiration, which then becomes the most direct path to hypocrisy and evil. As with Hegel's dutiful hypocrites, the "higher and purer" the ostensible goal that people like Hollingsworth have "surrendered themselves" to, and the more "unselfishly" they think they pursue it, the deeper they fall into self-deception in a vicious spiral that can be arrested only by drastic and radical intervention, providential or otherwise. For Hollingsworth, it is the trauma of Zenobia's death that brings him back to himself—to his true self, now guilt-ridden but essentially good, the self Zenobia had fatally fallen in love with.

Her tragic fate can be attributed in great measure to the stereotypically feminine self-deception of refusing to acknowledge the faults of the man she loves, even while paradoxically demonstrating her awareness of them. Thus after exposing Hollingsworth's hypocrisy, only to be ruthlessly cast aside by him, Zenobia replies to Coverdale's bitter charge that Hollingsworth is a "wretch" with a "heart of ice" by "turning haughtily" on Coverdale and refuting, with desperately illogical arguments, the case against her former lover that she has just established. "It was my fault, all along, and none of his. I see it now!" she continues, the feverish spontaneity of her vision underscoring the absurdity of her assertion, "He never sought me. Why should he seek me? What had I to offer him?" (p. 255). Poor Coverdale is too upbraided to supply the obvious answer: money, fame, brains, beauty, and true love, in that order of attractiveness to the egoistic prison reformer. Besides, Coverdale has already tried breaking through her infatuation with Hollingsworth, with no more success than he had in breaking through Hollingsworth's infatuation with himself: all he ever gets from Zenobia is a dressing-down. "She had shown me the true flesh and blood of her heart," he comments on her treatment of him in the Boston flat, "by thus involuntarily resenting my slight, pitying, half-kind, half-scornful mention of the man who was all in all with her" (p. 166). That he describes her resentment as involuntary demonstrates his recognition that she, no less than the man whose self-deception she so unarguably exposed, is a self-deceiver. Not only does she refuse to accept what she herself has established about him, but she is also unaware of her own true feelings toward him.

Several critics (and most readers, if my experience teaching the novel is anything to go by) explain away Coverdale's misgivings regarding Zenobia's honesty and integrity by insisting that we are really supposed to think him in love with Zenobia, consciously or not, despite the notorious declaration of his love for Priscilla on the last page.[3] Such an approach has led critics up some bizarre avenues, such as diagnosing Coverdale as sexually maladjusted[4] and even speculating that he might really be Zenobia's murderer.[5] Another line of thinking, proceeding from a feminist perspective, does not so much question Coverdale's motives as reject his analysis of her actions—that she would kill herself over Hollingsworth—as simpleminded.[6] Against this, though, it might be held that if Zenobia is said to deceive herself concerning her true feelings for Hollingsworth and then to turn against herself (instead of against him or Priscilla) in violent anger, such an account would not be sexist but would rather constitute a vivid illustration of how sexism operates in heterosexual relationships in a sexist culture. In fact, it is precisely such a pattern that R. B. de Sousa, in a feminist study of self-deception, identifies as belonging to a class of "self-deceptive emotions" that particularly affect women.[7]

But it is true that Coverdale can be harsh on her for her bad faith. At one point he "malevolently" describes her as "passionate . . . not deeply refined, incapable of pure and perfect taste" (p. 165). He instantly takes it back, but whether his observation is malevolent or not, it would yet appear that everything she does that might be construed as morally wrong is directly motivated by her hunger for the potent Mr. Hollingsworth. Primarily, this means abusing Priscilla as a potential, then as an actual competitor for his attention. It begins the very first time they meet, when Hollingsworth scolds Zenobia for her churlishness toward the girl and Zenobia meekly apologizes (pp. 28–29). It continues when she sticks a "weed of evil odor and ugly aspect" in Priscilla's hair. "There was a gleam of latent mischief—not to call it deviltry—in Zenobia's eye," observes Coverdale of the stinkweed incident, "which seemed to indicate a slightly malicious purpose to the arrangement" (p. 59). Later he catches her almost literally staring daggers as the younger woman and the man step into "the dimness of the porch" (p. 78). Then there is the sadistic storytelling episode, at the conclusion of which, as Fogle notes, Zenobia "further adds an unruffled and mocking hypocrisy" by feigning compassion for her helpless victim.[8] And so on. To be sure, we're much closer to childish naughtiness than to crimes of passion, and indeed a Freudian interpretation practically suggests itself: the two women engage in sibling rivalry without knowing that they are sisters, with Hollingsworth of course as the strong father figure neither ever had, and Zenobia doubling on the side as a surrogate mother for Priscilla.[9] (Such thinking also draws support from the girls' lack of a last name and the authoritarian male's lack of a first name.) For our purposes, however, it is necessary to accept no more than that Zenobia betrays her better nature because of sexual desire and jealousy, with or without the Freudian undertones.

Her picking on Priscilla is not terribly serious, but another evil deed to which her passion incites her is: her suicide. To say that she kills herself out of jealousy is not to ignore other motives, in particular her resentment of the oppression by society of any woman who, as she puts it to Coverdale at their final meeting, "swerves one hair's breadth out of the beaten track" (p. 224). No explicit connections are made between this more or less political motive and her personal frustrations; both, however, may be related to the special forms of self-deception to which women are liable owing to their position in the general culture. We have already noted her refusal to accept her own negative observations concerning Hollingsworth; similarly, she seems incapable of coming to terms with the reality of her betrayal. Not only does she exonerate Hollingsworth, but she tells Coverdale to give her jeweled flower to her rival, Priscilla, in a gesture that strikes Coverdale "as if she found a sort of relief in abasing all her pride" (p. 226). That her only response to jealousy is masochism, then self-destruction, might be accounted for by the double standard in jealousy that de Sousa examines in his study of self-deceptive emotions and sexism. Men can properly feel outraged by sexual betrayal and justifiably seek restitution by extreme measures, but women are supposed to repress their indignation, so that when a man overcomes his jealousy he may think of himself as nobly forbearing, while a woman's forbearance in the same situation would be an entirely internal matter from which she could derive no self-satisfaction. "This discrepancy adds yet another level of self-deception," de Sousa concludes, "namely that which results from the homonymy of 'jealousy,' that the task of achieving greater rationality of emotions is the same task for both" men and women.[10] Self-deceived by this "sexist mystification" into believing there is no alternative, Zenobia sacrifices first her flower, symbol of her sexuality, then her life.

The flower, by the way, is never mentioned again—we don't learn if Priscilla ever got it or, if she did, whether she wore it—which may be a mere oversight on Hawthorne's part, but the mystery of its disposition might also be meant to parallel Coverdale's uncertainty regarding Zenobia's state of mind at the instant of her death. Her corpse literally embodies her final ambivalence: the genuflecting knees suggest she was "reconciled and penitent," but the bent arms and clenched hands indicate "immitigable defiance" (p. 235). It was prescient of Hawthorne to intuit a feature of suicide that has since been clinically confirmed. In *The Savage God* A. Alvarez calls it "splitting" and points to instances of recovered would-be suicides telling of "some split-off part" of themselves that at the last moment decided not to die.[11] In terms of *The Blithedale Romance*, the tortured, self-divided appearance of her body is in keeping with the sexually generated (and sexist-conditioned) self-deceptions that have led to her ruin. Not a simple matter, as Coverdale recognizes even while comparing it to the stock situation of disappointed "village maidens" casting themselves into "the bosom of the old, familiar stream." He thereupon rhetorically asks, "Has not the world come to an awfully sophisticated pass, when . . . we cannot even put ourselves to death in whole-hearted simplicity?" (pp. 236, 237).

Priscilla shares with her half sister the self-deception concerning Hollingsworth's virtues, perhaps to an even greater degree. "So sure was she of his right," explains Coverdale, "that she never thought of comparing it with another's wrong." Zenobia has to explain away to herself and others her own accurate conclusions regarding his perfidy, but Priscilla never gets that far: "even Hollingsworth's self-accusation, had he volunteered it," wouldn't have altered what was for her "the one principle at the centre of the universe," that "Hollingsworth could have no fault" (pp. 220, 221). Even at the end, when Hollingsworth, with "self-distrustful weakness," is engaged in expiating those dreadful faults he now at last admits, Priscilla displays the same "deep, submissive, unquestioning reverence" as ever (p. 242). No matter what he does, she stays loyal: presumably, had he married an un-disinherited Zenobia, she would gladly have scrubbed the floors in his model prison. It is a bit much to swallow, and I'm inclined to agree with those who, beginning with Henry James, don't think Priscilla merits much consideration. For my purpose it is enough to say that Coverdale recognizes in her behavior self-deceptive emotions toward Hollingsworth—specifically, a refusal to apprehend the manifest truth about him—similar to those he identifies in the behavior of her sister.

The point is that Coverdale recognizes and identifies hypocrisy and self-deception wherever he sees them, and in this he is unique among Hawthorne characters, most of whom either are oblivious to this kind of falsehood or, as with the Phoebes and Pearls, react instinctively to it without comprehending what it is. Elsewhere in the fiction, only the omniscient Hawthornian narrator has an equivalent knack for and obsession with speaking of characters in these terms. To be sure, Coverdale sometimes sounds like such a narrator, especially with minor characters, as when he describes Westervelt as "a moral and physical humbug" (p. 95) or Moodie/Fauntleroy as "the man of show" (p. 193). Coverdale, however, is most emphatically a character as well as a narrator, and his attitude toward the self-deceptions of the three people he loves has the flavor not of authorial detachment but rather of personal involvement and direct engagement.

Yet there is more than personal involvement to Coverdale's attitude toward hypocrisy and self-deception, and by extension to Hawthorne's attitude in this book. To understand and full appreciate his attitude, we must at last confront a crucial issue: Coverdale's own good faith or bad faith.

The critics have not by and large thought much of his integrity, seeing him as, at best, a failed artist with a lukewarm temperament, and at worst as "a sort of intellectual vampire," to use Henry James's phrase which, however, he applied not to Coverdale but to recollections of Hawthorne by certain Brook Farm veterans. "Certainly, if Hawthorne was an observer, he was a very harmless one," James replied to the criticism,[12] and the refutation presumably would also apply to Zenobia's similarly motivated attack on Coverdale for his "insolent curiosity," "meddlesome temper," and "cold-blooded criticism" (p. 170). Modern readers tend to accept James's identification of author with narrator and therefore see Zenobia's accusation as an expression of Hawthorne's discomfort with his own novelistic methods. Thus Hyatt H. Waggoner regards Coverdale as "a critical, ironic, even hostile self-portrait of an aspect of Hawthorne that he wished to reject."[13] That negative aspect involves a sense of observing human affairs without participating in them and exploiting suffering for artistic ends. Edgar A. Dryden extends this line of thinking with ingenuity by interpreting the love-confession for Priscilla as a self-deceiving maneuver on Coverdale's part to evade the thrust of Zenobia's charge by making his "interest in the affairs of his three acquaintances" appear in retrospect to have been "personal rather than purely aesthetic or voyeuristic." "The bad faith involved in such a procedure is obvious," comments Dryden, linking Coverdale's bad faith with the failure of his narrative to arrive at a "sense of rebirth."[14] According to this view, Coverdale might well be thought of as a self-deceiving hypocrite: he pretends to himself and to others that his reasons for joining Blithedale and interacting with his fellow communards are altruistic and even motivated by romantic love, whereas in fact his intentions are selfish. Zenobia gives him the plain truth, with no admixture of the self-deceptive forbearance she accords that other egoist she exposes, Hollingsworth. Crews goes so far with such an approach as to speculate that Coverdale's self-deception, which he likens to that of James's unnamed narrator in *The Sacred Fount,* is a calculated gambit by Hawthorne: "he partially rescued a doomed story by stressing the principle of self-delusion inherent in the narrator's—and ultimately in his own—prying concern with other lives."[15] That would imply that the manner of its telling has only a fortuitous relationship to the story that is told and was not even an important part of its conception. Coverdale's self-deception, according to this view, is an afterthought.

I believe all such conclusions are seriously mistaken: Coverdale is neither a hypocrite nor a self-deceiver at the time he is actually telling his story, although he may now regard himself as having been either or both at the time of the events he is describing. But his attitude toward his past self-deception is one of understanding and tolerance. Take, for example, his retrospective feelings toward the hopelessly utopian idealism of the Blithedale experiment: his nostalgia is rather like that of some middle-aged former student protesters of the 1960s. "Whatever else I may repent of," he exclaims near the outset, "let it be reckoned neither among my sins nor follies, that I once had faith and force enough to form generous hopes of the world's destiny—yes!—and to do what in me lay for their accomplishment" (p. 11). Beneath the gentle self-mockery there sounds a note of genuine pride. Blithedale may well have been "an illusion, a masquerade, a pastoral, a counterfeit Arcadia" (p. 21), but Coverdale is by no means ashamed that he was once idealistic enough to have believed in it: "I rejoice that I could once think better of the world's improvability than it deserved" (p. 20). Compared to Hollingsworth's obsession with visiting his reforms upon the world whether it wants them or not, Coverdale's attitude, both then and now, is tolerant and generous. Although well aware of the commune's essential flaw—that people were pretending to be what they weren't—and while accepting responsibility for his participation in the sham, he places his errors in perspective, as when he admits he might justly have been "soundly cuffed" for "secretly putting weight upon some imaginary social advantage" in his ostentatiously egalitarian comportment with Silas Foster (p. 25). It was, however, not his intention of being Foster's equal that was hypocritical but rather the spirit in which he pursued it, which was not really egalitarian. Even so, he may be too hard on himself in censuring his earlier hypocrisy, inasmuch as the extent to which he succeeded in overcoming class barriers is indicated by Silas Foster's having been the only one who was distraught by Coverdale's departure: so vehemently did he fulminate and act as if it was good riddance (pp. 137–38) that we could infer his underlying regret at losing a friend. The inference was soon confirmed by the invitation he extended to Coverdale at the end of the chapter, "while giving my hand a mighty squeeze," to come back for a pork dinner (p. 144). By Yankee standards this was a handsome gesture of affection and acceptance, especially when contrasted with Foster's very first words to the Blithedale recruits: "Well, folks, . . . you'll be wishing yourselves back to town again, if this weather holds!" (p. 18). The prophecy belatedly came true with Coverdale, but Foster was hardly as satisfied as he would have been had he detected nothing but hypocrisy and condescension in Coverdale's attitude toward him.

The Blithedale experiment is a failure in terms of changing the world, but it succeeds in changing Coverdale, and for the better. It changes him physically from an effete weakling to a disciplined, capable workingman, who can jokingly boast (though not without real vanity) about his "muscular development" while engaged in the act of "lifting a big stone and putting it into its place" (p. 129). He can put things in their places not only because of his new muscles but also because of his new self-confidence. In fact, he has experienced a sort of rebirth: symbolically he died and was reborn when the cold he caught en route to Blithedale developed into something "like death," from which he emerged, in "literal and physical truth," as "quite another man" (p. 61). Nor does he ever entirely lose this spirit of regeneration, for at the end of the book, even though his life may have amounted to nothing, he still is idealistic enough to offer what remains of it—only half-seriously, it is true, but also only half-jokingly—to the cause of "Hungarian rights" (pp. 246–47). Again I think of a former draft card burner ready to go to jail in protest against a new war. "He confesses to a want of earnestness, but in reality he is evidently an excellent fellow," James remarks on the Hungarian rights passage, "to whom one might look, not for any personal performance on a great scale, but for a good deal of generosity of detail."[16]

The essential good faith of his attachment to the ideals of Blithedale is related to the more complex but ultimately well-meaning nature of his emotions toward his three friends. He acknowledges the half-truth of Zenobia's indictment, that his "cold tendency" to "pry" may have "gone far towards unhumanizing my heart." But he immediately counters that his attitude toward all three should be described as having "too much sympathy, rather than too little." The problem is, he explains with frank simplicity, that "a man cannot always decide for himself whether his own heart is cold or warm" (p. 154). His apprehension of our lamentable incapacity to understand ourselves, or to understand anyone else, is what gets in the way of Coverdale's deriving happiness from life, because he is too honest with himself to ignore it and yet, at the time of the events he is relating, he sees no way to overcome or transcend it. Thus he says to Priscilla, "If we could look into the hearts where we wish to be most valued, what should you expect to see? One's own likeness, in the innermost, holiest niche? Ah, I don't know! It may not be there at all." He calls this message the "bitter honey" it cost him "nearly seven years of worldly life" to learn (p. 76). Priscilla doesn't seem to have the least idea what he is talking about, and yet it is asserted that, like Coverdale, she too has powers of insight into unpleasant buried truths: "Hidden things were visible to her, . . . and silence was audible" (p. 187). In that case she must be unconsciously hypersensitive, like Phoebe Pyncheon, although unlike Phoebe she never demonstrates her visionary talents: even the prophecy about Blithedale that the Veiled Lady gives Coverdale at the very beginning of the book is left unspecified and, for all we know, unfulfilled (p. 6). It is Coverdale, not Priscilla, who demonstrates a greater than average insight, and he is fully conscious of "that quality of the intellect and the heart, which impelled me (often against my own will, and to the detriment of my own comfort) to live in other lives, and . . . to learn the secret which was hidden even from themselves" (p. 160). His painful inability to know whether his own heart is warm or cold, and his equally painful compulsion to look into the hearts of others, are two sides of the same "quality of the intellect and the heart," and his private tragedy is that he yearns for emotional involvement but cannot get beyond his accurate though (for him) emotionally devastating perception of the inevitable limitations of all human sympathies.

"It is really impossible to hide anything, in this world, to say nothing of the next," he tells Zenobia "with a secret bitterness"—

131

with another taste of bitter honey. "All that we ought to ask, therefore, is, that the witnesses of our conduct, and the speculators on our motives, should be capable of taking the highest view which the circumstances of the case may admit" (p. 163). This is virtually a mirror image of the advice we are meant to derive from Dimmesdale's experiences, which was that we should strive for other people to think the worst of us. Both pieces of advice are equally impossible to take. Zenobia wisely informs Coverdale that he is asking too much, that such a sympathetic understanding of our hidden natures must be left to "angels." She later demonstrates that other human beings, unlike angels, usually take precisely the lowest view of our conduct and our motives to which the circumstances may admit when she puts down Coverdale as an egoistic hypocrite. Admittedly, Coverdale provokes her by once again rubbing her face in Hollingsworth's preference for Priscilla, but Zenobia's reaction is extreme: she says Coverdale's "idea of duty" really comes from "motives" as "miserable" as she can think of, up to and including "a most irreverent propensity" to usurp the role of "Providence" (p. 170). Her jealous passion has blinded her to the good in Coverdale as well as to the evil in Hollingsworth.

In a recent article Keith Carabine rejects the usual negative presentation of Coverdale by critics, at whose hands, as at Zenobia's, he is "mistrusted and maligned," whether as a heartless snoop, an out-and-out liar, or a mediocre artist. Carabine seeks to give Coverdale a "sympathetic hearing" by concentrating on the narrative process, and he concludes that *The Blithedale Romance* is, in part, about the education of Coverdale into an acceptance of the role of the artist as a sympathetic observer who "misses out on life."[17] A key passage for Carabine is the following, in which Coverdale reflects on his "singularly subordinate" role in "these transactions": "It resembled that of the Chorus in a classic play, which seems to be set aloof from the possibility of personal concernment, and bestows the whole measure of its hope or fear, its exultation or sorrow, on the fortunes of others, between whom and itself this sympathy is the only bond. Destiny . . . chooses . . . the presence of at least one calm observer. It is his office . . . to detect the final fitness of incident to character, and distil, in his long-brooding thought, the whole morality of the performance" (p. 97). Coverdale unwillingly becomes a chorus to the tragedy enacted by the other three, but it is also important to keep in mind that he subsequently becomes the author of the relation of what he witnessed. I would press even harder than Carabine on the connection between Coverdale the participant and Coverdale the narrator by proposing that the same quality in Coverdale's personality that keeps him separated from the people he most cares for also informs the manner in which he tells his story. His painful awareness of the inherent limits of human understanding and compassion prevents him from getting close to people and to life, and his distance from life leads him to distance both himself and his readers from his narration of it. He achieves the distancing through the conscious and deliberate use of irony. Irony is the only positive response open to someone who has not been granted an inspired faith in an ultimate transcendence of human limitations and yet is too honest with himself to pretend that those limitations can be borne without pain.

In characterizing Coverdale as an ironist, I am proposing something different from the opinion that "Hawthorne had to invent the Jamesian narrator before James," a conclusion that, John Caldwell Stubbs assures us, "all post-Jamesian critics have noted."[18] The error in making this assumption is that it places the irony outside Coverdale and attributes it to Hawthorne alone, who is seen as manipulating the narrative in a manner beyond his purported narrator's comprehension, like James in *The Sacred Fount.* But this ignores frequent and significant manipulations of the narrative by Coverdale himself. Such manipulations on Coverdale's part are conscious and deliberate although they are never quite made explicit, for to make them explicit would detract from his purpose in adopting a manipulative technique in the first place, which is to keep the pain of human life at a supportable distance through irony.[19]

In saying earlier that beginning with *The Scarlet Letter* the emphasis slowly shifts from the moral to the ontological dimension of hypocrisy, I might almost have said equally that the emphasis shifts from hypocrisy to irony. It is in almost precisely these terms that hypocrisy is distinguished from irony by Kierkegaard. Superficially at least hypocrisy and irony seem rather close. Both the ironist and the hypocrite consciously create and deliberately maintain a discrepancy between appearance and reality in order to further a set of hidden goals. But as Kierkegaard distinguishes them, hypocrisy belongs to the "moral sphere" because "the hypocrite constantly strives to seem good though he is evil." Irony, on the other hand, "belongs to the metaphysical [I would say "ontological"] sphere, for the concern of the ironist is merely to seem other than he actually is." Yet irony is not merely a distinct quality from hypocrisy: in a real sense it is for Kierkegaard the only alternative. "As philosophers claim that no true philosophy is possible without doubt," he writes quite bluntly, "so . . . no authentic human life is possible without irony." It is my reading of *The Blithedale Romance* that Coverdale, by means of his narrative, attempts to achieve authenticity through irony. It is a difficult, even a dangerous project that he undertakes, and it is far from certain whether we can say he succeeds. Kierkegaard stresses that the authenticating properties of irony can be realized only if irony has been "mastered"; for those who do not "know" it, irony is something to be "feared"—and "woe to him who cannot tolerate the fact that irony seeks to balance the accounts!"[20]

I contend that Coverdale would indeed have something to be concerned about when irony seeks its balance because he has literally and deliberately tampered with his account of the events he narrates. I have already mentioned the poetic but implausibly accurate forecasts the major characters make almost simultaneously of their individual destinies. To take a similar but even more blatant example: early in the book Coverdale tells us that "once"—precisely when is shrewdly unspecified—he "whispered" to Hollingsworth that Zenobia "is a sister of the Veiled Lady," and also that if she were to lose the flower she wears in her hair "she would vanish, or be transformed into something else." When Zenobia tries to find out what Coverdale was saying about her, Hollingsworth answers: "Nothing that has an atom of sense in it" (p. 45). The irony, of course, is that both statements have nothing but sense in them, although none of the three characters, and the reader least of all, could have known it at the time. Zenobia is in fact Priscilla's sister, and after giving Coverdale her flower (when it, rather than she, has been transformed into something else, namely an item of jewelry), she will vanish from the world. That Coverdale reports this conversation as factual and never, either at that point or later, marvels at its uncanny prescience, whether coincidental or mystical, can reasonably be taken to mean only one thing: that the conversation is entirely a product of Coverdale's imagination, and

he has no qualms about the reader's eventually realizing this.

He doesn't mind having the reader discover that he has manipulated reality, not because he is willing to be considered either a liar or an unreliable narrator (had the term been available to him), but because he wants the reader to understand that by ironic distortions such as this one he can come much closer to conveying the true significance of his experience than he could have by mechanically adhering to mere factual accuracy. Thus after boring Hollingsworth with a long fantasy on the legendary ways in which they and the other communards will be imagined by their successors in the far future, he replies to Hollingsworth's objection that (as before) everything he says is nonsense: "I wish you would see fit to comprehend . . . that the profoundest wisdom must be mingled with nine-tenths of nonsense; else it is not worth the breath that utters it" (p. 129). The statement is valuable, not as a past communication from Coverdale the communard to Hollingsworth (on whom it would have been lost), but as a present communication from Coverdale the memoirist to his readers. He wishes his readers to comprehend that ironic nonsense and profound truth are inextricable. Kierkegaard's distinction between the ironist and the hypocrite, in morals and "metaphysics," is applicable to Coverdale as narrator: he manipulates the truth, but his purpose in doing so is not inherently evil. He has something valuable to say, and yet he knows that uttering it would be a waste of breath without a strong admixture of irony.

The largest group of manipulations contributes to what perhaps should be regarded as a sustaining metaphor: life as theater. Hawthorne launches the leitmotif in his own person in the Preface when he asserts that his reason for drawing on his Brook Farm experiences is "merely to establish a theatre . . . where the creatures of his brain may play their phantasmagorical antics" (p. 1)—a conceit that Coverdale comes close to duplicating when he laments "that, while these three characters figured so largely on my private theatre, I . . . was at best but a secondary or tertiary personage with either of them" (p. 70). For Hawthorne, of course, the play unfolds entirely within his brain, whereas Coverdale's "private theatre" exists on two levels: in the reality of his past personal life and in his present attempt at an imaginative recreation of that past reality. He confuses the two levels, deliberately, to make an ironic statement. His comparing himself to a classic chorus, already mentioned, adds to the idea: the chorus is both commentator and witness, and it is both detached from the action ("aloof," "calm") as well as involved. The cumulative effect of Coverdale's theatrically phrased observations is to convey not only his past apprehensions (that is, how he felt at the time) but also his present anxieties as the tragedy again unfolds on his page. Peering Jimmy Stewart–like into the boarding-house window across the back alley of his hotel, he marks the absence of only Hollingsworth and Moodie "to complete the knot of characters" that "had kept so long upon my mental stage, as actors in a drama," and he watches with "a positive despair" and begins "to long for a catastrophe." Were a catastrophe to come, he reports himself as having been thinking, he would then "look on," as "understandably" as he was able, "and, at all events, reverently and sadly. The curtain fallen, I would pass onward with my poor individual life" (pp. 156, 157). Zenobia sees him and the window curtain falls literally, but also metaphorically, "like the drop-curtain of a theatre, in the interval between the acts" (p. 159). Soon it will rise on the catastrophe he longs for. He longs for it because he knows it is coming; perhaps he knew in some premonitory sense in the past, but now he knows definitively, authorially.

Weaving theatrical metaphors into the texture of his narrative would be unremarkable were it not that he also manipulates purportedly real events to enhance their metaphorical effectiveness. The emphatically "literary" turn he gives to his reminiscences has been noticed before,[21] but not his self-conscious restructuring of reality, his deliberate setting of life and art into an ironic counterpoint. That is to say, not only do his retrospective comments bring out the theme of life as theater, but characters on his figurative stage say and do things effectively directed toward the same end. His very first dialogue with Zenobia is interrupted by "some one" asking, "Have we our various parts assigned?" (p. 16). Of course they have, but not at the time: only later, after the play is over, in Coverdale's narration—a paradox that the anonymous inquiry both underscores and subverts by the very implausibility of its having been made. Similarly, Coverdale has himself respond to Hollingsworth's asking what he does "in life" by saying, "Nothing, that I know of, unless to make pretty verses, and play a part, with Zenobia and the rest of our amateurs, in our pastoral" (p. 43). Distinguishing Zenobia's performance by calling the others "amateurs" is consistent with a subsidiary motif: Zenobia is a consummate actress, so perfect a performer that she is almost a "hypocrite" in the classical sense of *being* the mask she wears. Or perhaps we should think of her (in terms of Diderot's essay on acting) as being more genuine in her conscious role-playing than are the supposedly sincere nonperformers who applaud her.[22] Her deliberate theatricality brings out everyone else's unconscious feigning, just as her mere "presence" is said to turn all Blithedale into "a masquerade, a pastoral . . . in which we grown-up men and women were making a play-day" (p. 21). The histrionic metaphors attached to Zenobia can be found both in retrospect (through the narration) and in an ironic present through artfully contrived manipulations. At least twice Coverdale mentions her potential for a brilliant stage career (pp. 44, 106). "What an actress Zenobia might have been!" agrees Westervelt at her funeral, whereupon he characteristically turns truth into a lie by adding, "It was one of her least valuable capabilities" (p. 240). Rather, it was the source of all her worth. The first time her name is brought up, Coverdale explains—ironically, to her own father—that "Zenobia" (the name) is "a sort of mask in which she comes before the world" (p. 8). After futile efforts to penetrate the mask, he learns to accept it, along with the name, as the only reality. Torn between taking her "truest attitude" as the way she appears in town or the way he remembers her from Blithedale, he concludes that in "both, there was something like the illusion which a great actress flings around her" (p. 165).

"It is genuine tragedy, is it not?" Zenobia asks him at the start of their final scene together. She goes on to describe the "ballad" he should make of it, in the process delivering what becomes in the narrative her swan song. "As for the moral," she advises, "it shall be distilled into the final stanza, in a drop of bitter honey" (pp. 223, 224). This last phrase is an especially arch bit of dovetailing on the part of Coverdale, who, as we already saw, has used it earlier in describing his philosophy to the uncomprehending Priscilla. His message of "bitter honey" then, we recall, was that we never can be sure of seeing ourselves in the hearts of those we love, and therefore it is unwise to be "so very merry in this kind of a world" (p. 76). Thus Coverdale the narrator has Zenobia unknowingly allude to the dark moral her tragic destiny will fulfill. Thus Coverdale the ironist transcends the superficial implausibility, even impossibility, of his narrative in order to convey the deeper truth of his experience.

The deeper truth is that human beings can never know who or

what they really are, not even in love, and if not in love then nowhere. It is more than novelistically appropriate that the message should be unconsciously confirmed by a character who has theatricality and illusion at her essence, and whose inability to overcome her confusion of illusion and reality in her emotional life leads to her destruction. Moreover, her confirmation of the truth flies in the face of her ignorance: if she knew what she was saying she would also know that her self-destruction is unnecessary. But the very point is that she does not know what she is saying: her speaking the truth can only be taken ironically. Only in irony can the pain and loss she represents be borne by the creator of the narrative in which her story is related.

Does the creator of that narrative achieve authenticity through irony? In Kierkegaard's terms, has he mastered irony and come to know it, or should he fear that irony will come to balance the accounts? There are moments when the irony seems nearly out of control, especially in the "Masqueraders" chapter, when Coverdale writes that he is forced to flee the spectacle "like a mad poet hunted by chimaeras" (p. 211). It is not the men and women in costume who are chimerical, or rather it is not their costumes that make them so, because they, like all of us, are always wearing masks of one kind or another. What hunts Coverdale is the madness latent in his own poetic vision. But he escapes the reckoning that his resort to irony had led him into by a further recourse to irony. He compares himself to a poet pursued by the unreal, which is an ironic comparison par excellence, because that is just what he is as he writes those words: an artist pursued by his own imagined world. The author of the metaphor of the poet hunted by chimeras is nothing if he is not a man hunted, or haunted, by the unreality he has created in the very process of making the metaphor.

There is only one direction, then, in which to flee from hypocrisy and self-deception, and that is the direction of art. In moving in that direction, we do no more than exchange uncertainty about the nature and integrity of our inner selves for uncertainty about the truth of existence. Perhaps it is but a negligible gain, but at least the shift from morality to ontology makes life more tolerable. Coverdale's advice that we should not be "so very merry in this kind of a world" also means that we should not be so very sad in it either, and that advice applies whether the "kind of a world" we are talking about is the kind that some would maintain really exists or the kind that Coverdale's words actually refer to. That world, of course, is the kind that exists between book covers. (Coverdale's Blithedale, it might be added, and Hawthorne's *Blithedale Romance* are in this sense both the same thing.) Coverdale's good faith is ironic because it depends on his acceptance of the impossibility of good faith, which in turn sanctions his poetic exploitation of the ultimate impossibility of distinguishing reality from illusion and life from art. Hawthorne's full realization of this latter impossibility through Coverdale's narrative can largely be understood as the outcome of his long and exhaustive investigation, through his fiction, of hypocrisy and self-deception.

The Marble Faun
and Authorial Bad Faith

Perceptive readers will have observed that in my discussion of *The Blithedale Romance* I all but ignore the final sentence of the novel: Coverdale's notorious "confession" that he was in love with Priscilla. Frankly, I find the sentence an embarrassment, although not, as those who disagree with me perhaps might wish to propose, an embarrassment to my thesis regarding the nature of Hawthorne's fiction. Quite the contrary, it is well in keeping with the practice of a writer whose oeuvre could be characterized as a prolonged and often profound brooding on the human capacity for deception that he would end a novel with what purports to be a surprising revelation of a character's hitherto concealed innermost motive. Unfortunately, in this case the motive so revealed explains little or nothing about the character who reveals it. Rather—and this is what I feel is embarrassing—the revelation is most explicable not with regard to the literary character concerned but rather in terms of the extraliterary purposes of the novelist.

The final sentence is best understood as a miniature equivalent of the escape from seriousness that occurs in the final chapter of *The House of the Seven Gables*. In effect, it is a one-sentence surprise sunny ending. We had taken Coverdale to be a man who has learned a tragic lesson about the painfulness of life, a lesson we too might learn if we are able to emulate his honesty and summon his fortitude. Now we are told that Coverdale's entire problem is that he fell in love with someone who did not love him back. That, obviously, is easier to live with. For whatever reasons (professional? personal?), Hawthorne wishes his readers to close the book heaving

140

a sigh not only of pity but also of relief. Perhaps he would hold that for a self-proclaimed writer of romances to produce such a result is obligatory. I would not push this too far, but it is possible that in calling the last chapter "Miles Coverdale's Confession" instead of "My Confession" he is giving his less sentimental readers permission to construe the final words as the author's epilogue to his romance rather than the narrator's conclusion of his purported memoir. It is even possible (though admittedly questionable) to read into Coverdale's confession an apology on the author's part for including it. "As I write it, he [the reader] will charitably suppose me to blush, and turn away my face" (3:247), writes Hawthorne, conceivably in acknowledgment that he shares my embarrassment over the passage. (After all, Coverdale had exhibited other intimate aspects of his emotional life without blushingly apologizing for doing so.) My speculation, if correct, would hardly be to Hawthorne's credit. Indeed, it would be tantamount to accusing him of deliberately misleading the reader and misguidedly destroying the integrity of his own work into the bargain.

This brings up the intriguing issue of Hawthorne's honesty as a writer. The matter has been raised before, most sweepingly in an interesting though at times oblique recent essay by Jeffrey L. Duncan, who claims that all through his career Hawthorne is "a self-confessed, self-proclaimed dissembler," comparable in his dissembling to Dimmesdale, who is "a liar and a lie."[1] Most commentators who operate along these lines, however, reserve most of their criticisms for Hawthorne's final period, and his last completed novel in particular. A good example is Crews, who objects to "the prevailing air of self-contradiction" in *The Marble Faun* arising from "insincere" characterization, most notably in the case of Miriam, on whom Hawthorne "prefers to vent" his "sexual nausea."[2] More recently Dauber has attacked not just the characterization but virtually everything in the book, even the descriptions of the setting, for "basic dishonesty" and "bad faith." What he means is that Hawthorne has convinced himself that he is telling a story when he really has no story to tell. He is merely posing as a storyteller while deceiving himself into accepting the validity of the false pose he strikes. "The author, trying on various attitudes, comes to accept them as fact. What he asserts, he unthinkingly believes." Events, people, objects, even the landscape are "fundamentally factitious" because the true though hidden purpose of their being included is nothing more than to point vapid morals or produce picturesque effects. We end with a "pseudostory" or a "travelogue," epitomized for Dauber by Donatello's vapid little fable.[3]

Those who would defend Hawthorne from this sort of accusation appeal to the main themes of the novel, which concern the relation of art to life or of illusion to reality, and declare that what seems to be bad faith in Hawthorne's artistry is actually a fully intended and indeed valuable statement on the nature of art. The most straightforward use of this tactic of transforming apparent defects into virtues is made by Stubbs. Disabusing us of "the idea of probing deeply into the psychological motivation of the characters" as in the earlier fiction, Stubbs compares *The Marble Faun* to "modern expressionistic novels" in which psychological portraiture is secondary to making an artistic statement. Acknowledging that the people in Hawthorne's book are "barely distinguishable from the art objects around them," he argues that this is consistent with their function.[4] Similarly, he might well answer Dauber that the landscape seems factitious because it is in fact meant to be seen as artificial.

Baym adopts a more complex version of the same overall approach in her attempt to absolve Hawthorne of the charge of "trying duplicitously to conceal his meanings." On the contrary, the apparent subversion of art derided or explained away by the other critics becomes the starting point of Baym's thesis that the "purport of *The Marble Faun* was that great or serious art was no longer possible." As she reads the story, Kenyon is "a truly promising artist" who is persuaded by the prudish Hilda into accommodating his work to "modern society," which is based on "a great hypocrisy about human nature." Thus at the center of the book is Kenyon's tragedy, "a tragedy for modern art."[5] For reasons that are not strictly relevant to my present concerns I cannot go along entirely with this reading;[6] but I fully share the perception that artistic failure is at the essence of what the book has to offer. Dryden goes even further in this direction by suggesting that Hawthorne has come to the same conclusion concerning art in general that Hilda reaches in the novel when she loses her enthusiasm for the old masters. She discovers that the "core of meaning" she once thought she could see in the paintings is in fact only "the result of a mystification."[7] Furthermore, the narrator attributes

Hilda's disillusionment not so much to the character's growth from innocence to maturity as to the moral inadequacy of the artists she mistakenly admired, specifically with regard to their insincerity. They "essayed to express to the world what they had not in their own souls" (4:338).

I cannot help finding something distasteful, like sour grapes, in Hawthorne's indictment of art. To the extent Baym's interpretation holds up—that is, if Hawthorne does in fact contend that society is too hypocritical for great art to survive—then the contention is annulled by his own previous achievements, because it is precisely the pervasiveness of hypocrisy and bad faith that has provided him with the materials for making great art. Moreover, the same materials are in plentiful supply in *The Marble Faun*. Indeed, the continuities of characters and situations are so pronounced that he must at some point have been planning a novel on the same pattern as his earlier work. That a good novel does not emerge should be ascribed to the failure of the artist, not to the failure of art. I believe that in back of the failure we can detect the same retreat from seriousness that flaws *The House of the Seven Gables* and mandates that Coverdale append his gratuitous confession to *The Blithedale Romance*. In *The Marble Faun* the far more pernicious consequence of Hawthorne's taking the easy way out is a general creative paralysis affecting most of the book because this time he gives up the struggle early on. Having assembled the makings for what might have been his most serious novel, Hawthorne scarcely begins to write it.

I say it might have been his most serious novel because *The Marble Faun* is unique in Hawthorne's fiction for including the only instance of one human being deliberately taking the life of another. This is an extraordinarily low homicide rate for a major noncomic storyteller. Here it is the major incident, or at least the main catalyst of the action, although it is symptomatic of the author's refusal to follow through that the murder becomes less and less significant an event as the narrative progresses. Admittedly it would be unfair to fault Hawthorne for not having written *Crime and Punishment*. Yet the expectation of the reader, especially of the reader who has read Hawthorne's earlier work, would be to observe the psychological processes an almost childishly undesigning man would be subjected to after impulsively killing an evil hypocrite. That is more or less what is promised by the situation established in the first part of the novel. But it is hardly what Hawthorne delivers. To argue that instead he delivers a statement on art is beside the point and even perverse if what is meant is that he is justified in disregarding the claims of his own art because his message is that all art is a sham anyway.

One reason it becomes inevitable that the murder will fade into triviality is the unvarying dehumanization or demonization of the victim. Many readers object to the reptilian status into which Chillingworth descends at the end of *The Scarlet Letter*, but at least in the early chapters his humanity is pathetically undeniable. Similarly, the narrator's savage taunting of the dead Judge Pyncheon is effective because the characterization of him (when alive) had been engrossing and believable, albeit satirical. But the creature destroyed by Donatello never passes the threshold of the recognizably human, not even as a caricature. At best he might be thought of as a sort of gargoyle. Hawthorne makes him the embodiment of the religious hypocrisy he finds everywhere he looks in Rome: "the pretence of Holiness and the reality of Nastiness" (p. 326). Rome is hypocrisy's world capital. He presents the city as literally resting on a foundation of putrefaction and bathed in an atmosphere of malaria. That sort of gross overstatement is effective in describing an urban landscape but counterproductive when applied to a person whose death is supposed to alter profoundly the lives of those who caused it. From the little we know about him, the monk's situation is curiously like that of Dante's monkish hypocrites insofar as he well knows just what he is, a damned hypocrite, and he feels awful about it and suffers over it, but to no avail. And that is pretty much where Hawthorne leaves it. That is also where Dante leaves it, but he is writing a metaphysical poem, whereas Hawthorne is writing a novel. Yet his only attempt to account for the dead man's behavior in understandably human terms comes near the end of the book, hundreds of pages after the murder, when we are told that he suffered from the "insanity which often developes in old, close-kept breeds of men" (p. 431). In other words, his subhuman personality is explicable on the basis of degenerate racial characteristics. It is sad that Hawthorne should sink so low.

Even without a substantive victim the novel might still have succeeded in fulfilling the expectations it raises regarding the psychology of the killer and his quasi accomplice. The murder is skillfully described in such a way that it is unclear to what extent or in what manner Donatello and Miriam knew what they were doing or even what they were thinking. Irrational action as a philosophical issue goes back to Aristotle; moreover, it is closely related to self-deception, as a recent study by David Pears makes clear.[8] So it would seem likely that Hawthorne might pursue some such approach. I believe he may have started out trying to do so, especially in the brief scene where Donatello in effect blackmails Miriam by threatening to kill himself if she denies that she gave her "whole consent" to the crime, which leads the reader to wonder if it can be said that either of them did. But the paradox of motivated irrationality, to borrow Pears's phrase, is soon dropped. Donatello and Miriam accept their guilt equally as though they had acted with full premeditation, and Hawthorne shifts into his less promising "transformation" theme concerning Donatello's tedious progress from extrovert to penitent.

It may make as little sense to ask why Hawthorne did not write the novel he had started to write as it would to ask why his career as a whole ended in irresolution and artistic collapse. The two questions may even be the same: why did Hawthorne not continue to develop his fiction in the same general direction as before? why was he incapable of building on his earlier triumphs? To answer by remarking that inspiration deserted him or his powers failed him, of course, merely begs the question, which, however, does not mean it is not the right answer or at all events the only answer possible. Another formulation of the circular response is that he ran out of things to say. He did indeed run out of things to say about hypocrisy and self-deception, but what he had already discovered about them, and especially about the latter, certainly could have formed the basis for additional novelistic explorations of the intricacies of human affairs. Arguably Hawthorne's discoveries about self-deception in fact did to a large extent form the basis for the novelistic explorations of the intricacies of human affairs undertaken by Henry James.

For what it is worth, allow me to conclude by offering my own tentative explanation, in terms of the conclusions I have reached in this book, for Hawthorne's apparent inability to proceed. I have argued that the ontological aspect of hypocrisy and self-deception eventually came to predominate over the moral aspect in his fiction by a process that in retrospect seems natural and inevitable. But the   145 process may also in some sense have been irreversible. That is to say, having arrived at the point where, as in *The Blithedale Romance*, an ontologically grounded irony is the only way out of the moral indeterminacy faced by man in all his "deluded generations," to continue along the same path would necessarily require leaving the moral dimension further and further behind. To be more specific, having created Coverdale and his unsettling but clear-sighted perspective, Hawthorne could not return to the world of *The Scarlet Letter,* in which it is still possible for characters to make unironic moral choices, even if those choices remain ineluctably and excruciatingly uncertain. But if he could not return, neither could he go on: he was too imbued with the moral sensibility, even though his own genius had placed him in a position such that movement away from morality was the only avenue of productivity open to him. Instead of going forward, he attempted to move sideways into the less challenging quarters of romance—a fictionalized travelogue, a gothic inheritance plot—but regrettably these detours led him nowhere.

Notes
Index

Notes

INTRODUCTION
"The Age of Hypocrisy"

1. Judith Shklar, "Let Us Not Be Hypocritical," *Daedalus* 108 (1979): 8–10. This essay is reprinted in Shklar's *Ordinary Vices* (Cambridge: Harvard Univ. Press, 1984).

2. G. W. F. Hegel, *The Phenomenology of Mind*, 2d ed., trans. J. B. Baillie (London: George Allen & Unwin, 1931), p. 669. For more on Hegel's abhorrence of hypocrisy, see Judith N. Shklar, *Freedom and Independence: A Study of the Political Ideas of Hegel's Phenomenology of Mind* (New York: Cambridge Univ. Press, 1976), pp. 192–93.

3. Jonathan Robinson, *Duty and Hypocrisy in Hegel's Phenomenology of Mind: An Essay in the Real and Ideal* (Toronto: Univ. of Toronto Press, 1977), p. 2.

4. See, for example, Lionel Gossman, *Men and Masks: A Study of Molière* (Baltimore: Johns Hopkins Univ. Press, 1963), pp. 128, 136; Henri Peyre, *Literature and Sincerity* (New Haven: Yale Univ. Press, 1963), pp. 51–52; A. J. Krailsheimer, *Studies in Self-Interest from Descartes to La Bruyere* (Oxford: Clarendon Press, 1962), pp. 112–13; Jean Starobinski, "Montaigne on Illusion: The Denunciation of Untruth," *Daedalus* 108 (1979): 86.

ONE
Hypocrisy and the New England Way

1. See Gerhard Kittel, ed., *Theological Dictionary of the New Testament* (Grand Rapids: Eerdmans, 1964–76), 8:563–66.

2. D. W. Burdick, "Hypocrisy," in Geoffrey W. Bromley, ed., *International Standard Bible Encyclopedia* (Grand Rapids: Eerdmans, 1979), 2:790.

3. See Dante Alighieri, *The Divine Comedy*, trans. with a commentary by Charles S. Singleton (Princeton: Princeton Univ. Press, 1970), *Inferno* 2. Commentary, p. 399, n. on l. 92; Wallace Fowlie, *A Reading of Dante's Inferno*

(Chicago: Univ. of Chicago Press, 1981), p. 149; Thomas Aquinas, *Summa Theologiae* (London: Blackfriars, 1972), 41:175.

4. Lionel Trilling, *Sincerity and Authenticity* (Cambridge: Harvard Univ. Press, 1973), p. 16.

5. Anthony Palmer, "Characterising Self-Deception," *Mind* 88 (1979): 50.

6. Raphael Demos, "Lying to Oneself," *Journal of Philosophy* 57 (1960): 588. Examples of attempts to circumvent the paradox would start with Demos himself in the same article and proceed through a long list. The most successful, in my opinion, is Herbert Fingarette: I discuss his *Self-Deception* later. The flattest denial of the conceivability of self-deception comes from M. R. Haight, *A Study of Self-Deception* (Sussex: Harvester, 1980), particularly pp. 108–19.

7. Two contemporary avowals that self-deception is intrinsically evil are Demos, "Lying to Oneself," p. 591, and T. S. Champlin, "Self-deception: A Reflexive Dilemma," *Philosophy* 52 (1977): 297. Equally forthright denials that it is *always* evil include: Jeffrey Foss, "Rethinking Self-Deception," *American Philosophical Quarterly* 17 (1980): 242; and Bela Szabados, "The Morality of Self-Deception," *Dialogue* 13 (1974): 25. Yet more recently David Pears, treating self-deception in the wider context of irrationality in general, not only affirms the "good effect" that self-deception may have in certain cases, but even discusses the virtues of what he calls "self-deceptive faith" (*Motivated Irrationality* [Oxford: Oxford Univ. Press, 1984], pp. 33–36). A new book is devoted entirely to this issue: Mike W. Martin, *Self-Deception and Morality* (Lawrence: Univ. Press of Kansas, 1986).

8. Matthew Arnold, *St. Paul and Protestantism* (New York: Macmillan, 1902), p. 68; Fyodor Dostoyevsky, *The Brothers Karamazov*, trans. Constance Garnett (New York: Modern Library, n.d.), p. 48.

9. For a critical view of the Sartrean theory of bad faith see Haight, pp. 53–72. The best study of Freud and morality remains Philip Rieff, *Freud: The Mind of the Moralist* (New York: Doubleday, 1961), which, however, has little to contribute on the topic of self-deception per se.

10. Francis Bacon, *Works*, ed. James Spedding et al. (Boston, 1861), 14:89. I quote the English translation of 1598.

11. See Frank Whigham, *Ambition and Privilege: The Social Tropes of Elizabethan Courtesy Theory* (Los Angeles: Univ. of California Press, 1984), pp. 98–99.

12. John S. Coolidge, *The Pauline Renaissance in England: Puritanism and the Bible* (Oxford: Clarendon Press, 1970), p. 89.

13. Ibid., p. 91n.

14. Ibid., pp. 90–91.

15. Excerpted in Perry Miller and Thomas H. Johnson, eds., *The Puritans: A Sourcebook of Their Writings* (New York: Harper & Row, 1963), 1:314–15.

16. Edmund S. Morgan, *Visible Saints: The History of a Puritan Idea* (New York: New York Univ. Press, 1963), p. 65.

17. Cf. Coolidge, *Pauline Renaissance*, p. 65n.

18. See, for example, Everett H. Emerson, *John Cotton* (New York: Twayne, 1965), pp. 136–37.

19. Miller and Johnson, *The Puritans*, 1:315.

20. Coolidge, *Pauline Renaissance,* p. 135.

21. Quoted in Ernest Benson Lowrie, *The Shape of the Puritan Mind: The Thought of Samuel Willard* (New Haven: Yale Univ. Press, 1974), pp. 182–83.

22. Phyllis M. Jones and Nicholas R. Jones, eds., *Salvation in New England: Selections from the Sermons of the First Preachers* (Austin: Univ. of Texas Press, 1977), pp. 91, 94.

23. Thomas Shepard, *The Parable of the Ten Virgins* (London, 1660), p. 128. I have omitted some italics in the original. I consulted this edition on microfilm.

24. See Morgan, *Visible Saints,* pp. 100–101, 114, 134.

25. Michael McGiffert, ed., *God's Plot: The Paradox of Puritan Piety, Being the Autobiography and Journal of Thomas Shepard* (Amherst: Univ. of Massachusetts Press, 1972), pp. 104, 42.

26. This particular passage can be found more conveniently in the excerpt from Shepard's *Parable of the Ten Virgins* anthologized in Jones and Jones, *Salvation in New England,* p. 137.

27. McGiffert, *God's Plot,* pp. 17–18.

28. Shepard, *Parable of the Ten Virgins,* pp. 149, 150.

29. Ibid., p. 128.

30. See Michael J. Colacurcio, *"Gods Determinations Touching Half-Way Membership:* Occasion and Audience in Edward Taylor," *American Literature* 39 (1967): 307–9.

31. Quoted in Norman Petit, *The Heart Prepared: Grace and Conversion in Puritan Spiritual Life* (New Haven: Yale Univ. Press, 1966), p. 210.

32. See Allan Heimert, *Religion and the American Mind* (Cambridge: Harvard Univ. Press, 1966), pp. 310–15, 503–4.

33. Two recent studies taking such an approach are Philip F. Gura, *The Wisdom of Words: Language, Theology, and Literature in the New England Renaissance* (Middletown: Wesleyan Univ. Press, 1981), and Mason I. Lowance, Jr., *The Language of Canaan: Metaphor and Symbol in New England from the Puritans to the Transcendentalists* (Cambridge: Harvard Univ. Press, 1980).

34. Norman S. Fiering, "Will and Intellect in the New England Mind," *William and Mary Quarterly,* 3d ser., 29 (1972): 549–50.

35. Henri F. Ellenberger, *The Discovery of the Unconscious: The History and Evolution of Dynamic Psychiatry* (New York: Basic Books, 1970), p. 537, and cf. Trilling, *Sincerity and Authenticity,* pp. 141–44.

36. I see no reason to get involved in the interminable debate as to what Hawthorne's religious beliefs were, or if he had any. I am willing to think of at least the younger Hawthorne as a "literary Calvinist" in Gene Bluestein's sense of the term. See his " 'The Brotherhood of Sinners': Literary Calvinism," *New England Quarterly* 50 (1977): 195–213.

TWO

Tales and Sketches: The Enigma behind the Mask

1. See David Perkins, *Wordsworth and the Poetry of Sincerity* (Cambridge: Harvard Univ. Press, 1964), p. 38.

2. In one particularly striking passage he argues (against Coleridge) that even a man who adopted the motto of Milton's Satan and willed himself to evil would still be thwarted by "revivals of his better nature" (William Wordsworth, *Prose Works*, ed. W. J. B. Owen and Jane Worthington Smyser [Oxford: Clarendon Press, 1974], 2:113).

3. All citations of Hawthorne's writings are from *Works*, Centenary Edition, ed. William Charvat et al. (Columbus: Ohio State Univ. Press).

4. For the Greek mask, see, for example, Albert Cook, *Enactment: Greek Tragedy* (Chicago: Swallow Press, 1971), p. 37; Donald J. Mastronarde, *Contact and Discontinuity: Some Conventions of Speech and Action on the Greek Tragic Stage* (Berkeley: Univ. of California Press, 1979), p. 114; and Walter F. Otto, *Dionysus: Myth and Cult* (Bloomington: Indiana Univ. Press, 1965), p. 89. Regarding the No, see Akira Kurosawa's comment that "the actor becomes the man whom the mask represents," in Roger Manvell, *Shakespeare and the Film* (New York: Praeger, 1971), p. 103.

5. Newton Arvin, *Hawthorne* (Boston: Little, Brown, 1929), p. 186.

6. Neal Frank Doubleday, *Hawthorne's Early Tales: A Critical Study* (Durham: Duke Univ. Press, 1972), p. 155.

7. Jeremy Taylor, *Ductor Dubitantium; or, The Rule of Conscience in All Her General Measures*, 2d ed. (London, 1671), pp. 17–18.

8. See, for example, Arvin, *Hawthorne*, p. 61, and Robert H. Fossum, *Hawthorne's Inviolable Circle: The Problem of Time* (Deland: Everett, Edwards, 1972), pp. 2–3.

9. Frederick C. Crews, *The Sins of the Fathers: Hawthorne's Psychological Themes* (New York: Oxford Univ. Press, 1966), pp. 64, 69.

10. See Doubleday, *Hawthorne's Early Tales*, p. 164.

11. Cf. ibid., p. 168.

12. Cf. ibid., p. 167.

13. Crews, *Sins of the Fathers*, pp. 111, 106–7 and n.

14. Reinhold Niebuhr, *The Nature and Destiny of Man: A Christian Interpretation* (New York: Charles Scribner's Sons, 1951), p. 207.

15. Nicholas Canaday, Jr., "Hawthorne's Minister and the Veiling Deceptions of Self," *Studies in Short Fiction* 4 (1966): 135–42.

16. Michael J. Colacurcio, "Parson Hooper's Power of Blackness: Sin and Self in 'The Minister's Black Veil,'" in *Prospects*, vol. 5, ed. Jack Salzman (New York: Franklin, 1980), pp. 331–411, 376.

17. Nina Baym, "The Head, the Heart, and the Unpardonable Sin," *New England Quarterly* 40 (1967): 43n.

18. Nina Baym, *The Shape of Hawthorne's Career* (Ithaca: Cornell Univ. Press, 1976), pp. 117–18.

19. Leonard J. Fick, *The Light Beyond: A Study of Hawthorne's Theology* (Westminster: Newman, 1955), p. 139.

20. Shepard, *Parable of the Ten Virgins*, p. 128.

21. Roy R. Male, *Hawthorne's Tragic Vision* (Austin: Univ. of Texas Press, 1957), p. 86.

22. Doubleday, *Hawthorne's Early Tales*, pp. 205–9.

23. See Morgan, *Visible Saints*, pp. 2–3 and n.

24. Quoted in Coolidge, *Pauline Renaissance*, p. 61.

25. Fossum, *Hawthorne's Inviolable Circle*, p. 54.

THREE

The Scarlet Letter: A World of Hypocrites

1. Allen Austin, "Satire and Theme in *The Scarlet Letter*," *Philological Quarterly* 41 (1962): 508–11.

2. Richard Harter Fogle, *Hawthorne's Imagery: The "Proper Light and Shadow" in the Major Romances* (Norman: Univ. of Oklahoma Press, 1969), p. 34.

3. A. Robert Lee, " 'Like a Dream behind Me': Hawthorne's 'The Custom-House' and *The Scarlet Letter*," in Lee, ed., *Nathaniel Hawthorne: New Critical Essays* (London: Vision Press, 1982), p. 66.

4. Hyatt H. Waggoner, *Hawthorne: A Critical Study* (Cambridge: Harvard Univ. Press, 1963), p. 134.

5. Nicholas Canaday, Jr., " 'Some Sweet Moral Blossom': A Note on Hawthorne's Rose," *Papers on Language and Literature* 3 (1967): 186–87.

6. Baym, *Shape of Hawthorne's Career*, p. 130.

7. Gary Lane, "Structural Dynamics and the Unknowable in *The Scarlet Letter*," in C. E. Frazer Clark, Jr., ed., *The Nathaniel Hawthorne Journal 1977* (Detroit: Bruccoli Clark, 1980), pp. 325–26.

8. Crews, *Sins of the Fathers*, p. 126; Allan Lefcowitz, "*Apologia* pro Roger Prynne: A Psychological Study," *Literature and Psychology* 24 (1974): 37.

9. Sacvan Bercovitch, *The Puritan Origins of the American Self* (New Haven: Yale Univ. Press, 1975), p. 242 n. 57.

10. See, for example, Bruce Ingham Granger, "Arthur Dimmesdale as Tragic Hero," *Nineteenth-Century Fiction* 19 (1964): 202.

11. Nina Baym, Introduction to *The Scarlet Letter* (New York: Penguin, 1983), p. 18.

FOUR

Arthur Dimmesdale: The Hypocrite Saint

1. Herbert Fingarette, *Self-Deception* (London: Routledge & Kegan Paul, 1969), pp. 138–39, 140, 142.

2. Henry James, *Nathaniel Hawthorne* (New York: Harper & Brothers, 1907), pp. 110–11.

3. Kenneth Dauber, *Rediscovering Hawthorne* (Princeton: Princeton Univ. Press, 1977), p. 111.

4. Charles Feidelson, Jr., "*The Scarlet Letter*," in Roy Harvey Pearce, ed.,

153

Hawthorne Centenary Essays (Columbus: Ohio State Univ. Press, 1964), pp. 60–61.

5. Fingarette, *Self-Deception*, p. 140.

6. William B. Dillingham, "Arthur Dimmesdale's Confession," *Studies in the Literary Imagination* 2 (1969): 24.

7. Edward H. Davidson, "Dimmesdale's Fall," *New England Quarterly* 36 (1963): 358.

8. Darrel Abel, "Hawthorne's Dimmesdale: Fugitive from Wrath," *Nineteenth-Century Fiction* 11 (1956): 101, 102.

9. Terence Martin, "Dimmesdale's Ultimate Sermon," *Arizona Quarterly* 27 (1971): 238–40.

10. Nina Baym, "Hawthorne," in *American Literary Scholarship 1971*, ed. J. Albert Robbins (Durham: Duke Univ. Press, 1973), p. 31.

11. Male, *Hawthorne's Tragic Vision*, p. 116.

12. Austin Warren, *"The Scarlet Letter:* A Literary Exercise in Moral Theology," *Southern Review* 1 (1965): 40.

13. Michael Wigglesworth, *Diary, 1653–1657*, ed. Edmund S. Morgan (Gloucester: Peter Smith, 1970), pp. 52–53.

14. For some brief but provocative insights into Dimmesdale's sexuality, see Nicholas Canaday, "Another Look at Arthur Dimmesdale," *C.E.A. Critic* 41 (1979): 13–16.

15. Michael Small, "Hawthorne's *The Scarlet Letter:* Arthur Dimmesdale's Manipulation of Language," *American Imago* 37 (1980): 121.

16. Ernest W. Baughman, "Public Confession and *The Scarlet Letter,"* *New England Quarterly* 40 (1967): 542, 541.

17. Thomas Shepard, *The Sound Believer*, excerpted in Jones and Jones, *Salvation in New England*, pp. 65–68.

18. Michael J. Colacurcio, "Footsteps of Ann Hutchinson: The Context of *The Scarlet Letter,"* *ELH* 39 (1972): 493.

19. Baughman, "Public Confession," p. 543.

20. Jonathan Edwards, *Basic Writings*, ed. Ola Elizabeth Winslow (New York: New American Library, 1966), pp. 174–75.

21. Thomas Aquinas, *Summa Theologiae*, 41:175. For Thomas Aquinas, hypocrisy is not a mortal sin so long as the hypocrite retains a "regard for holiness" (p. 181 and note C).

22. Miller and Johnson, *The Puritans*, 1:150.

23. Frederick Newberry, "Tradition and Disinheritance in *The Scarlet Letter,"* *ESQ* 23 (1977): 3.

24. Ibid., p. 20.

25. Jeffrey L. Duncan, "The Design of Hawthorne's Fabrications," *Yale Review* 71 (1981): 70.

26. John Updike, "On Hawthorne's Mind," *New York Review of Books*, March 19, 1981, p. 41.

FIVE

The House of the Seven Gables:
Judge Pyncheon and His Brotherhood

1. Thomas Pynchon, *Slow Learner: Early Stories* (Boston: Little, Brown, 1984), p. 5.

2. Richard Gray, " 'Hawthorne: A Problem': *The House of the Seven Gables,*" in Lee, *Nathaniel Hawthorne*, pp. 104–5.

3. Baym, *Shape of Hawthorne's Career*, pp. 169, 166.

4. Nina Baym, "Hawthorne's Holgrave: The Failure of the Artist-Hero," *Journal of English and Germanic Philology* 69 (1970): 586.

5. Male, *Hawthorne's Tragic Vision*, p. 136.

6. Fogle, *Hawthorne's Imagery*, pp. 75–76.

7. Cf. Taylor Stoehr, "Hawthorne and Mesmerism," *Huntington Library Quarterly* 33 (1969): 57.

8. Marcus Cunliffe, "The House of the Seven Gables," in Pearce, *Hawthorne Centenary Essays*, p. 98.

9. James, *Nathaniel Hawthorne*, p. 125.

10. Ralph Waldo Emerson, "Self-Reliance," in Stephen E. Whicher, ed., *Selections* (Boston: Houghton Mifflin, 1957), p. 161.

11. See J. Eugene Wright, Jr., *Erikson: Identity and Religion* (New York: Seabury Press, 1982), p. 166.

12. Baym, *Shape of Hawthorne's Career*, p. 159.

13. James, *Nathaniel Hawthorne*, p. 124.

14. See, for example, Benjamin Boyce, *The Polemic Character, 1640–1661* (Lincoln: Univ. of Nebraska Press, 1955), p. 68.

15. Crews, *Sins of the Fathers*, p. 182.

16. Gray, " 'Hawthorne: A Problem,' " p. 103.

17. Arvin, *Hawthorne*, p. 193.

18. Arvin, *Hawthorne*, pp. 193, 194.

19. Male, *Hawthorne's Tragic Vision*, p. 134.

20. Crews, *Sins of the Fathers*, p. 175.

21. Richard Harter Fogle, *Hawthorne's Fiction: The Light & the Dark* (Norman: Univ. of Oklahoma Press, 1964), p. 158.

22. Shepard, *Parable of the Ten Virgins*, pp. 154, 123.

23. Ibid., p. 156.

24. Shklar, "Let Us Not Be Hypocritical," pp. 15–18.

25. See Marion L. Kesselring, *Hawthorne's Reading, 1828–1850* (New York: New York Public Library, 1949), p. 47.

26. Quoted in Pierce W. Gaines, *William Cobbett and the United States, 1792–1835* (Worcester: American Antiquarian Society, 1971), p. xiv.

27. John W. Osborne, *William Cobbett: His Thought and His Times* (New Brunswick: Rutgers Univ. Press, 1966), p. 207; James Sambrook, *William Cobbett* (London: Routledge, 1973), p. 125.

28. Sambrook, *William Cobbett*, p. 125.

29. See Darrel Abel, "Hawthorne's House of Tradition," *South Atlantic Quarterly* 52 (1953): 570.

30. William Cobbett, *Sermons on Hypocrisy and Cruelty* (London, 1822), pp. 2, 110. Cobbett also has a sermon on sloth that might well have entered into the conception of the Pyncheon tendency to sluggishness.

31. Quoted in Jones and Jones, *Salvation in New England*, p. 113.

32. Quoted in Lowrie, *Shape of the Puritan Mind*, p. 112.

SIX

The Blithedale Romance: "The Dust of Deluded Generations"

1. Nicholas Canaday, Jr., "Community and Identity at Blithedale," *South Atlantic Quarterly* 71 (1972): 38.

2. Baym, *Shape of Hawthorne's Career*, p. 195.

3. A good example is Ellen E. Morgan, "The Veiled Lady: The Secret Love of Miles Coverdale," *Nathaniel Hawthorne Journal* 1 (1971): 169–81. I will discuss the love declaration for Priscilla further in my postscript.

4. Richard Van DeWeghe, "Hawthorne's *The Blithedale Romance:* Miles Coverdale, His Story," in Clark, ed., *Nathaniel Hawthorne Journal, 1977*, pp. 289–303.

5. John Harmon McElroy and Edward L. McDonald, "The Coverdale Romance," *Studia Neophilologica* 14 (1982): 1–16.

6. Mary Suzanne Schriber, "Justice to Zenobia," *New England Quarterly* 55 (1982): 61–78.

7. R. B. de Sousa, "Self-deceptive Emotions," *Journal of Philosophy* 75 (1978): 692–93.

8. Fogle, *Hawthorne's Fiction*, p. 176.

9. Cf. Crews, *Sins of the Fathers*, pp. 202–4.

10. De Sousa, "Self-deceptive Emotions," p. 694.

11. A. Alvarez, *The Savage God: A Study of Suicide* (New York: Random House, 1972), pp. 111–12.

12. James, *Hawthorne*, p. 85.

13. Hyatt H. Waggoner, *The Presence of Hawthorne* (Baton Rouge: Louisiana State Univ. Press, 1979), p. 111.

14. Edgar A. Dryden, *Nathaniel Hawthorne: The Poetics of Enchantment* (Ithaca: Cornell Univ. Press, 1977), pp. 102–3.

15. Crews, *Sins of the Fathers*, p. 196.

16. James, *Hawthorne*, p. 129.

17. Keith Carabine, " 'Bitter Honey': Miles Coverdale as Narrator in *The Blithedale Romance*," in Lee, *Nathaniel Hawthorne*, pp. 110–11, 117.

18. John Caldwell Stubbs, *The Pursuit of Form: A Study of Hawthorne and the Romance* (Urbana: Univ. of Illinois Press, 1970), p. 136.

19. Claudia D. Johnson also recognizes that the story is told from an "intricate, ironic point of view"; she attributes this, however, to Coverdale's evil penchant to lie and distort, so that the entire narrative is thus "sick, false, destructive, and self-serving . . . a deceptive fabrication by a damned soul" (*The Productive Tension of Hawthorne's Art* [Univ. of Alabama Press, 1981], pp. 84, 83). It seems incredible to me that Hawthorne could be imagined placing such a character at the center of a full-length romance as the first-person narrator.

20. Søren Kierkegaard, *The Concept of Irony with Constant Reference to Socrates* (London: Collins, 1966), pp. 273, 338–39, 340. For another contrast between hypocrisy and irony see D. C. Muecke, *The Concept of Irony* (London: Methuen, 1969), p. 22.

21. See, for example, Crews, *Sins of the Fathers*, pp. 197–98.

22. Cf. Denis Diderot, *The Paradox of Acting*, trans. Walter Herries Pollock (New York: Hill and Wang, 1957), p. 51.

POSTSCRIPT
The Marble Faun and Authorial Bad Faith

1. Duncan, "Design of Hawthorne's Fabrications," pp. 53, 70.

2. Crews, *Sins of the Fathers*, pp. 218, 222.

3. Dauber, *Rediscovering Hawthorne*, pp. 212, 217, 218–19.

4. Stubbs, *Pursuit of Form*, p. 156.

5. Baym, *Shape of Hawthorne's Career*, pp. 250, 248, 249, 230, 231.

6. Briefly, while I agree that the Cleopatra statue sounds *to us* more interesting than the snow maiden, I can't help thinking that Hawthorne may have thought them equally worthwhile as hypothetical subjects, and therefore Baym's assumption that we are meant to detect an artistic sellout by Kenyon may not be warranted. I would raise similar objections to other places where Baym reads a negative value judgment into passages where I find none.

7. Dryden, *Poetics of Enchantment*, pp. 131–32.

8. Pears, *Motivated Irrationality*, pp. 15–40.

Index